# SOCCER:

## WINNING TECHNIQUES

by

### Joe Luxbacher, Ph.D.
Department of Health, Physical
and Recreation Education
University of Pittsburgh

D1195858

**eddie bowers publishing company**
2884 HICKORY HILL
DUBUQUE, IOWA 52001

# DEDICATION

To Ruth Kohlmyer. Her enthusiasm and love of the game has touched the lives of countless players, both young and old alike.

eddie bowers publishing company
2884 HICKORY HILL
DUBUQUE, IA 52001

ISBN 0-912855-66-5

Printed in the United States of America.

9 8 7 6 5 4 3 2 1

# ACKNOWLEDGMENTS

Completion of this book would not have been possible without the help and cooperation of a great many people. First and foremost, I would like to express my gratitude to the players and coaches with whom I've had the opportunity to share thoughts and experiences.

Many of the action photos which accompany the text were kindly provided by professional teams and former players of the North American Soccer League. My sincere appreciation also goes to Tina Galli for her expertise in preparing many of the skill demonstration illustrations.

Finally, I am greatly indebted to Francis Luxbacher, my first and finest coach. His comments and insight regarding the contents of this book were invaluable.

# INTRODUCTION

Soccer! The game provides a universal language, a common bond among peoples and nations that transverses political, cultural and religious barriers. From its origins in China to the modern day counterpart, soccer has served as a common focal point in the lives of countless millions. The emotion and excitement which surrounds the sport is unparalleled in the realm of competitive athletics.

The game has undergone a variety of changes throughout its long and colorful history. Rules governing play, philosophies and methodologies of coaching, and the tactical organization of players on the field — all have been characterized by a transient nature, with newer and more innovative methods evolving from the old. Despite these changes, one constant steadfastly remains as the primary driving force behind the efforts of the coach — the preparation of players, both individually and collectively, for optimal performance in match competition. It is with that theme in mind that this book is written.

# TABLE OF CONTENTS

# CHAPTER 1

# History of the Game

The sport of soccer, known as "football" throughout most of the world, has a rich and varied history. Although the actual origins of the game are difficult to substantiate, a variety of kick-ball games have been documented from earliest times. The original forerunner is believed to be an ancient Chinese game called "tsu chu" which was played as early as 2500 B.C., during the reign of Emperor Huang - Ti. Tsu chu, which involved kicking a stuffed ball made of animal skin, was played during festival-like celebrations and was also used for the training of soldiers. Historical references indicate that the game was played extensively during the Han Dynasty (206 B.C. to 220 A.D.).

Early forms of the modern game developed in other areas of the world as well. There is documentation that the Greek's played a football-type game called "episkyres" as early as 600 B.C. At about the same time the Roman empire played their own version of the sport and called it "harpustum". The Roman games often took place between rival towns several miles distant. The ball, usually the inflated bladder of an animal, was kicked, punched or carried with the town marketplaces designated as goals. The games often lasted several days with participants traveling across rugged terrain between towns. Both episkyres and harpustum were ball-carrying games, however, and actually combined the elements of soccer and rugby since use of the hands was permitted in propelling the ball. Although modern soccer can be considered a derivative of these ancient games, its growth was nurtured in medieval Britain.

Soccer in the British Empire was originally associated with the celebration of yearly festivals, and bore only a vague resemblance to the modern sport. Standardized rules did not exist and were not considered of particular importance. Regardless, the game quickly gained widespread popularity throughout Britain and soon play was no longer limited to holidays or festive celebrations. Soccer gradually began to touch the lives of people at all levels of society. Legend has it that, in 1349, King Edward III became so upset with his troops because they preferred to play soccer rather than engage in warfare that he prohibited play

*Soccer is enjoying widespread popularity as a collegiate sport.*

by the military. It is ironic that it was the British military which eventually played a major role in introducing the sport throughout the world during the late 1800's, a period when expansion of the British empire was at its zenith.

Soccer continued to flourish in the public school system of England and culminated with the founding of Sheffield Football Club in 1857, England's first soccer club. The original Sheffield Rules were adopted as the official laws governing play. Until that time the rules of play were somewhat flexible, usually dependent on the fancies of the players involved in any particular match. Use of the hands for controlling the ball was often permitted. The Sheffield Rules prohibited use of the hands, a major step in creating the initial differentiation between the sports of soccer-football and rugby-football. Even so, the basic rules of play still lacked uniformity throughout various areas of the country and it was not uncommon for teams to use as many as fifteen players per side. As a consequence a variety of playing formations were employed, depending on the number and style of players comprising the team. In 1870 a law was enacted restricting the number of players on the field to eleven per team at any one time. The adoption of that rule was an important step in the game's development, since it was the first attempt at organizing players into strategic systems of play.

Another significant event in the early history of the sport occurred in London when, in 1863, the Football Association was founded. Representatives of eleven clubs, all favoring the kicking form of the game, gathered at Freemason's Tavern and agreed to confine play entirely to kicking and heading. To differentiate between the two forms of football one was called rugby and the other associations football, later shortened to assoc and eventual-

*More than one million women are also playing in organized leagues.*

ly to soccer. As time passed the game spread beyond the confines of Great Britain, with the organization of the game in England providing a spark for growth in other countries as well. In 1867 the Buenos Aires Football Club was founded in Argentina, Association rules were first played in Germany in 1870, and the Scottish Football Association was organized in 1873. During the latter years of the 19th century many new associations were formed. An international governing body became a necessity, and in 1904 the Federation Internationale de Football Association (FIFA) first met and organized in Paris. Today there are more than 140 member nations of FIFA. Every four years participating countries compete in an international tournament to determine the champion of the soccer world. The World Cup, initiated in 1930, is considered by many to be the ultimate sporting spectacle with the games attracting a huge following from across the globe. Approximately one billion television viewers observed the last World Cup final.

The United States of America is a member nation of FIFA. Soccer has been firmly established here for more than a century, although only recently has the game enjoyed a period of tremendous popular growth. The sport was originally characterized by an ethnic orientation as immigrants brought the game from their homelands. Many towns and clubs organized and sponsored teams, oftentimes creating intense and long standing rivalries among neighboring villages. Soccer was also played on an informal basis at the college level as early as the 1850's. The first official college soccer match is reported to have been played between Princeton and Rutgers in 1869. A number of universities, primarily those located in the east, followed that lead and introduced soccer into their athletic curriculum during the latter part of the nineteenth century. As growth continued, both on the

3

*Soccer is the fastest growing youth sport in America.*

sandlots and in the schools, it became apparent that a national governing body was needed to unify the various leagues and associations. In 1913 the United States Soccer Football Association (USSFA) was organized and approved by FIFA. The name has since been changed to the United States Soccer Federation (USSF).

Millions of children are presently playing in organized leagues throughout the country. The rapid expansion of youth soccer necessitated the establishment of the United States Youth Soccer Association (USYSA) in 1974. The USYSA, an affiliate of the USSF, functions to develop, promote and administer the sport for players under 19 years of age.

High school and college athletic programs are beginning to reap the benefits of fan and player interest generated at the youth level. Each year more high schools are adopting soccer as a varsity sport. More than 500 NCAA (National Collegiate Athletic Association) affiliated colleges and universities sponsor varsity men's programs. Many schools belonging to the National Association of Intercollegiate Athletics (NAIA) also field highly competitive teams. In addition, the acceptance of women's soccer as a high school and collegiate sport has created many opportunities for young women to continue their active involvement as a playing participant.

The continued growth of soccer in America appears very promising. In the years ahead the game should enjoy even greater popularity as more and more people discover the benefits that the sport offers. We can realistically expect that, in the not so distant future, the United States will move to the forefront of the world soccer scene.

# CHAPTER 2

# Team Management and Organization

Coaching is an inexact science. There is no cookbook formula that will guarantee success, since each coaching situation is somewhat different from any other. It is therefore the responsibility of every coach to assess his or her own unique situation and react accordingly. Even though situations differ, however, all coaches should keep in mind several general guidelines which can be universally applied.

## GUIDELINES FOR COACHING YOUTH PLAYERS

### 1. Be organized.

There is no substitute for organization and correct preparation. A well conceived practice regimen will flow smoothly from beginning to end, players will remain active and enthusiastic throughout, and economical use of time will be achieved.

### 2. Consider players as individuals.

Although soccer is a team game the coach must deal with individual personalities. It is important to be flexible with regard to individual needs, strengths and weaknesses. The coach should strive to have players improve on weaknesses and progress according to their own ability levels. In doing so one must consider the player's stage of physical and mental development — individuals may be of the same calendar age but may differ in their biological age (i.e., physical and mental maturity).

### 3. Watch the training load.

Practices should be designed to challenge players, both physically and mentally. However, a training session that is too physically demanding is just as bad as one that is too easy. The philosophy of "more is always better" is not necessarily correct. The ultimate concern must be the quality rather than quantity of practice time. When structuring the training session, coaches should take into account the following:
- age of the player
- physical and emotional maturity
- environmental conditions (temperature, humidity, etc.).

### 4. Coach yourself.

Modeling can be a very effective learning tool. Coaches should practice the basic skills so as to become adept at demonstrating the correct techniques to their charges. In doing so they will gain an appreciation for the degree of difficulty experienced in achieving proper skill performance, and will acquire a more complete understanding of the challenge which confronts young players.

### 5. Simplify.

Much of the inherent beauty of soccer rests with the fact that it is basically a simple game. Let's keep it that way! Whenever possible use simple explanations. Avoid jargon and excessive rhetoric which serves only to confuse and bore players.

### 6. Don't overcoach!

Practice is for the players. The coach should not monopolize the training session with unnecessary talking and frequent stoppages of play. Briefly introduce the topic and then have players become physically involved. When an appropriate time for a "coaching point" occurs, activity should be stopped as the coach provides feedback on performance. However, don't belabor the point. Strive to keep players active and the practice flowing smoothly.

### 7. Make practice fun!

The innovative coach can use a variety of drills and fun — type competitions to make training sessions interesting and enjoyable. We should never lose sight of the fact that the primary reason for playing the game is the enjoyment derived from participation. Practice characterized by drudgery and monotony creates a poor learning environment.

## METHODOLOGY OF COACHING

Soccer is a demanding sport. Players must maintain a high degree of physical fitness, develop a mastery of the basic techniques, and acquire an understanding of the tactical concepts of team play. It is the responsibility of the coach to ensure that players receive adequate preparation in each of these areas. Efficient use of training time is essential in order to accomplish that aim. Practices should be structured so that fitness, skill, and tactical training occur simultaneously within the same drill or sequence of drills. For instance, an exercise designed to emphasize passing skills which also involves running and movement develops both technique and fitness, resulting in economical use of practice time. Coaches should strive to employ economical training methods. To do so requires advance planning and organization. It is imperative that the coach have a sufficient number of soccer balls available for training sessions, ideally one ball for each player. An ample supply of balls will permit all players to actively participate throughout duration of the practice, rather than having to wait their turn for an opportunity to use a ball.

## Fitness

Soccer players must develop a specific type of fitness, one that meets the physical requirements of match play. The coach must consider the following areas of concentration.

### 1. Flexibility and agility.

A variety of exercises can be used to increase the individual's range of motion. Players must be flexible in order to execute the specialized skill movements required for successful performance.

### 2. Endurance.

Two basic types of endurance — general and local — are required of all players. General endurance refers to one's cardiovascular fitness, their ability to sustain activity for an extended period of time. Local muscle endurance refers to the ability of a specific muscle, or group of muscles, to perform under the stress of fatigue.

Interval training is an efficient and economical method for developing both general and local muscle endurance. As the term "interval" implies, the activity alternates between periods of intense physical effort (work) followed by short periods of recovery (rest). The rhythm of interval training closely resembles the type of physical stress encountered during actual game play, with periods of intense activity interspersed with periods of lesser activity.

Another advantage of interval training is its flexible format. The intensity of the workout can be manipulated by adjusting variables in the work schedule. These variables include:
• intensity of effort during work interval
• length (time) of work interval
• number of repetitions of work interval
• length (time) of the rest interval
• activity (if any) during the rest interval

7

### 3. Speed

Speed is a complex concept. With respect to the game of soccer, it involves much more than straight-out sprinting speed. To improve a player's soccer specific speed, coaches should consider the following aspects.

• *Quick start* — Quickness over a short distance is more important than speed over a great distance. The ability to get off the mark quickly is very important.

• *Quick motion* — Deceptive movements which unbalance an opponent serve to increase one's soccer specific speed.

• *Skill* — Players who develop a high degree of skill will save themselves precious moments during game competition due to their ability to quickly control the ball.

• *Tactics* — The ability to read the game, to anticipate situations in advance and react accordingly, can sometimes compensate for a lack of foot speed. Through proper positioning players should try to avoid, as much as possible, situations where they will have to outrace a faster opponent in order to win the ball.

### 4. Strength and Power

It is a common misconception that soccer players do not need to train for strength and power. Strength training is accomplished by players working against some sort of resistance. The resistance can be applied in several ways; the players own body weight (push ups), resistance of a partner, or a basic weight training program.

## Technique (Skill) Training

Skill development should progress through a series of steps, beginning with the very basic and advancing to the more complex. The ultimate aim is that players will eventually be able to demonstrate skillful performance under the pressures of a game situation. However, as the saying goes, you have to walk before you can run. It is a mistake to initially place novice players in situations where they have little chance of experiencing success. They must first develop the correct technique of skill execution, in a relatively pressure-free learning environment, before they are required to perform the skills under match conditions. Technique training should occur through the following sequence of stages.

### 1. Foundation or Basic Stage.

The correct method of skill performance is demonstrated and players practice the basic movements. Development of

*Foundation (basic) stage of skill training*

correct technique is of the utmost importance. In this state players are not exposed to any type of pressure, and are performing the skills at half speed or slower.

### 2. Game-Related Stage.

Once players have mastered the basic technique, they should aspire to a higher standard of performance. In the game-related stage a variety of stressors are incorporated into the drills, stressors which increase the degree of difficulty encountered in achieving correct performance. Players must deal with the pressures of movement, repetition, fatigue, restricted space, and/or limited time, all realistic stressors which must be overcome in actual game conditions. Initially the pace should be approximately 80% of normal with a gradual increase to full speed.

### 3. Game-Condition Stage.

As the level of competence improves players are gradually subjected to actual gamelike conditions. Time and space are restricted even more and the ultimate form of game pressure, challenge from an opponent, is integrated into the exercises. In the game-condition stage players are functioning at full speed in a match situation.

*Individual tactics — the 1 vs 1 matchup.*

## Tactics

Players must acquire a high degree of tactical knowledge in order to make correct decisions in response to the ever changing situations encountered during play. Tactics, or team play, exist on three levels — individual, group and team.

An effective method of teaching individual and group tactics is through the use of the coaching grid. The coaching grid is an area which has been sectioned off by marker lines. Grids vary in size, but the typical area is 10 yards × 10 yards or 10 yards × 20 yards. Small group exercises (1 vs 1, 2 vs 1, etc.) can be conducted within the grid. The reduced area serves to limit the time and space available to players, and provides realistic match conditions. A series of grids can also be used for organizing large numbers of players into purposeful learning situations.

• *Individual Tactics* — Although soccer is a team game, players must be prepared for the frequent 1 vs 1 confrontations which inevitably occur during play. Individual attacking and defending responsibilities are of equal importance.

• **Group Tactics** — Players must be able to function in small groups since these situations constantly occur in the vicinity of the ball. Group tactics involve as few as three players (2 vs 1) and progress through situations as 2 vs 2, 3 vs 2, 4 vs 2 and 4 vs 3. Attacking and defending concepts should be emphasized, although not necessarily in the same exercise.

• **Team Tactics** — The aim of tactical training is to organize, both offensively and defensively, a coordinated team effort. Once players comprehend individual and group tactical concepts, the coach can successfully mesh the eleven individuals into a smooth functioning unit. Team tactics are the final stage of tactical development.

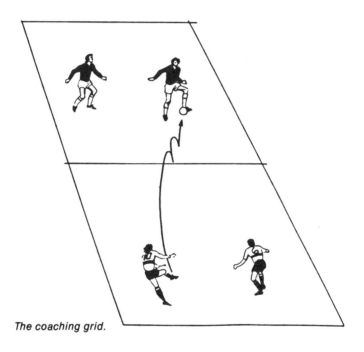

*The coaching grid.*

## ORGANIZATION OF PRACTICE SESSIONS

Effective organizational skills are possibly the most important qualities required for successful coaching. They are of particular significance when planning an effective training session. Although it is generally assumed that most coaches know how to structure a practice, actually there has been little written on the topic. The following guidelines are provided to aid coaches in developing a practice regimen.

### 1. Plan a realistic practice.

The coach must consider the age and abilities of his or her team members. Players should be challenged to achieve a higher standard of performance, but the challenge must not be so difficult that there is little chance of realizing success.

### 2. Develop a theme for the practice.

Each training session should be designed with a particular theme in mind. For instance, the general theme might be to improve passing skills. Don't attempt to cover too many topics in a single practice; rather, concentrate on one or two primary areas.

### 3. Develop a rhythm of practice.

Practice time should alternate between periods of high and low intensity work. Players may not be capable of working at maximum intensity for extended periods so the coach must plan accordingly. The training rhythm should reflect the type of activity patterns encountered in match play.

### 4. Develop a logical sequence.

Drills and small group situations should be organized to progress through a series of stages. Each step in the sequence should provide a foundation for the next stage, enabling a smooth transition from one drill to the next.

### 5. Employ economical training methods.

Exercises should be signed to incorporate elements of fitness, skill, and tactics into each drill. In addition, an ample supply of soccer balls, ideally one for each player, should be available.

### 6. Don't forget your goalkeeper.

The keeper needs practice in the skills and tactics required to play the position. Although goalkeepers will benefit from participating in drills which develop their field skills, a portion of each training session must be devoted to specialized goalkeeper training.

### 7. Coaching aids.

Through advanced planning the coach can anticipate which types of coaching aids will be useful in the training session. These may include such items as cones, flags, small goals, and scrimmage vests, to mention only a few.

**8. Always finish practice with a gamelike situation.**
    The objective of practice is to better prepare players for game competition. Each training session should therefore conclude with a game. It is not necessary that the game be a full-sided (11 vs 11) affair. Small-sided games, involving reduced numbers of players (4 vs 4, 5 vs 5, etc.), are actually more beneficial since players have the opportunity to touch the ball more often.

## SAMPLE PRACTICE FORMAT

    Coaches should plan practices according to the needs and abilities of their team members. Game competition will clearly demonstrate the strengths and weaknesses of a team, so the coach can usually structure training sessions based upon what the game dictates. As a consequence, the nature of practice sessions may vary from one team to the next, both in content and duration.
    The following is a sample of a typical practice schedule. The format is provided only as a general guideline, and should be adapted to address the specific needs of your team.

## PRACTICE:   THEME — IMPROVE TEAM INTERPASSING
### (Duration — 90 minutes)

**Warm-up Routine (15-20 minutes)**
    Prior to a strenuous training session players should undergo a warm-up period. Included in the warm-up are flexibility and agility exercises, light running with the ball, and drills designed to improve muscle strength and endurance. The innovative coach might devise some sort of "fun type" competition, involving movement as well as passing skills, to conclude the warm-up.

**Technique Training (20 minutes)**
    A variety of passing drills, progressing from basic to more complex, should comprise this portion of the session.

**Fitness Training (10 minutes)**
    Whenever possible, use of a soccer ball should be incorporated into the fitness training. For instance, players may be required to run sprints at maximum speed while dribbling the ball. Fitness training should be structured on an interval-type format.

### Break (5 minutes)

During the rest period be sure to have plenty of fluids available for players to replenish water lost through perspiration.

### Group Tactics (20 minutes)

Group passing exercises, emphasizing combination play and tactical movement, would be included in this portion of the practice.

### Small-Sided Games (20 minutes)

The final portion of practice is devoted to small-sided games (5 vs 5, 6 vs 6, etc.). The coaching emphasis is primarily on team interpassing and combination play.

### Warm-Down

Practice concludes with a short period of stretching and light flexibility exercises. During the warm-down, while players are relaxed and attentive, the coach summarizes the session and highlights important concepts.

## COACHING RESPONSIBILITIES DURING THE GAME

Most coaches are aware that their duties do not end on the practice field. Although most of the actual coaching is done prior to the start of a game, the coach must fulfill several important responsibilities during and immediately following each contest.

### 1. Know the line-up and substitutes.

The coach should have a general idea of when he/she plans to substitute, for whom, and under what conditions.

### 2. Observe the tactics of your opponent and adjust your own team's strategy accordingly.

Ensure that each player understands their role within the team structure.

**3. Enjoy the game!** Usually the coach cannot have a significant impact on individual player performance once the whistle sounds to start play. Preparation during the days and hours prior to the game is usually the determining factor. During the match the coach's comments should focus on team concepts in order to keep players well organized and disciplined in their play.

## 4. Post game duties.

Following the game it is the coach's responsibility to make sure that any injuries are properly treated. A short critique of the team's performance may be appropriate, but long winded discussions should be delayed until another day. Details concerning the time and place of the next practice or game should be announced.

# CHAPTER 3

# Player Equipment and Coaching Aids

One can play the game of soccer with a minimal amount of equipment. Shoes, shirt, shorts, socks and a ball are the basic requirements. The goalkeeper, due to the specific demands of the position, wears a specialized set of equipment that differs in some respects from the field players.

## EQUIPMENT — FIELD PLAYERS

### Shoes

A soccer player's shoes are his most prized possession, the tools of his trade. It is important to choose a shoe which is comfortable, light weight, and provides good traction. A variety of shoes are available, each designed for a specific type of playing surface.

Shoes with multistuded molded soles are popular since they can be used on both natural grass and artificial turf surfaces. The molded rubber cleats generally provide good footing in both wet and dry field conditions.

Screw-in studded shoes are most appropriate for soft, wet fields since the longer spikes provide added traction on such playing surfaces. The cleats are detachable and should be replaced at regular intervals as they begin to show wear and tear. The screw-in studs are not suitable for hard dirt surfaces or for synthetic turf.

Lightweight training flats, usually made of supple leather, are most appropriate for dry field conditions. They provide adequate traction on natural and synthetic surfaces, and enable the player to get a "feel for the ball" due to the soft, form fitting, leather. Training flats are not suitable for wet field conditions.

*From left to right: indoor training flat, synthetic turf shoe, screw-in studded shoe for soft natural surfaces.*

Synthetic turf shoes are designed specifically for artificial playing surfaces. The soles usually possess a large number of miniature molded studs or pebbles. Turf shoes can also be used on hard, dry playing surfaces such as grass or dirt.

## Balls

It is essential that each player have access to a soccer ball. Refinement of basic skill movements can be accomplished only through repetitive-type practice with a ball. A variety of soccer balls are available, ranging from low priced synthetic models to expensive hand sewn leather types. Three sizes are commonly used, depending on the age and physical development of the players. The regulation ball (size #5) for adult players is 27 to 28 inches in circumference and weighs 14 to 16 ounces. The size #4 ball is suitable for youth players, typically 6-10 years old, and is 25 to 26 inches in circumference and weighs 11 to 13 ounces. For the very young player there is an even smaller ball (size #3) which is 23 to 24 inches in circumference and weighs only 9 to 10 ounces.

## Uniforms

In addition to shoes, the basic uniform for field players consists of a shirt, shorts and socks. Choice of uniform is usually based upon cost, climate conditions under which games are typically played (hot, cold, humid, etc.), and fit (avoid restrictive material which inhibits player movement).

Soccer shorts and jerseys, both long and short sleeved, are available in many different styles and models. Cotton and nylon are the most commonly used fabrics due to their comfort, light weight, and durability. Socks also come in several varieties. The stirrup type (footless) sock, similar to those worn by baseball players, was commonly used in the past. Today the most popular type is the full-footed nylon model. The full-footed stocking is the best choice since shin guards fastened inside the sock will stay firmly in place.

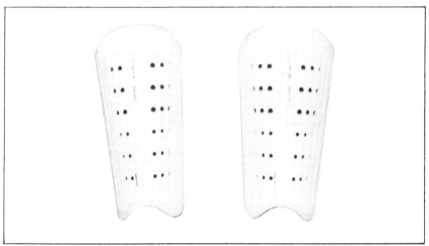

*Shin guards, although light in weight, provide adequate protection for the lower leg area.*

## Shin Guards

Shin guards are an essential part of every player's equipment. They are usually made of light, flexible plastic and most models are relatively inexpensive. Contrary to popular belief, wearing shin guards will not hinder players in their movements or ability to perform in the match. They will, however, prevent unnecessary injury to the lower leg.

## EQUIPMENT — THE GOALKEEPER

The goalkeeper is the one true specialist on the soccer field. He must perform a variety of skills and acrobatic movements that are different from those required of field players. As a consequence the keeper's equipment needs differ somewhat from his teammates.

Most goalkeeper's prefer a shirt that is long sleeved with protective padding at the elbows. The padding is lightweight and flexible so as not to inhibit movement. The Laws of the Game also require the keeper's shirt to be a different color than those of the field players.

Goalkeeper shorts are padded in the area of the hip joint to prevent injury when diving. Full length keeper pants are also becoming popular, especially for indoor soccer where the playing surfaces are very hard.

Many goalkeepers choose to wear specialized gloves, particularly when playing in unfavorable weather conditions. A variety of styles are available with each designed to aid in handling and controlling the ball. Most goalkeepers wear gloves at all times during indoor competition since they are required to field numerous shots, often from point blank range.

A variety of optional equipment is also available to the goal-keeper. Elbow and knee pads can be worn to provide added protection. Male goalkeepers may choose to wear a protective plastic cup to prevent injuries to the groin area. Finally, on days when bright sunshine may affect play, keepers can wear a baseball type cap to shield their eyes from the direct sunlight.

## COACHING AIDS

Various types of coaching equipment are available which will serve to enhance the training and development of players. Although most coaches do not have the luxury of possessing all of these aids, access to even a few can be very useful in practice situations.

### Cones or Flags

These can be used to mark off small fields or grids for practice purposes.

### Small Goals

Small portable goals are beneficial for use in small sided games on a less than regulation size field. Relatively inexpensive to construct, small goals can also be used for indoor soccer.

### Kickboard

A kickboard can be a very valuable addition to the training site. Repetition training of the basic skills, including passing, receiving, and shooting, can be accomplished through players using the kickboard surface as a target. Goalkeepers can also use the kickboard in refining their skills.

## Pendulum Ball

A ball suspended from a post by a rope can be used for practicing a variety of skills. It is especially effective in developing the techniques of heading, passing, and receiving balls.

## Scrimmage Vests

Different colored vests aid in differentiating between teams. Vests are necessary in order to avoid confusion among players when coaching group tactics or when playing small-sided games.

## Magnetic Board

A magnetic board, illustrating a soccer field with eleven moveable players, is an excellent visual aid for teaching group and team tactics.

*The magnetic soccer board can be very useful for illustrating tactical concepts.*

## Diving Pit

Providing a soft surface for goalkeeper training will prevent unnecessary injuries to the keeper. A pit filled with sand or saw dust serves as an excellent area for the development of correct diving technique.

## Audio Visual Equipment

Observing oneself on film can be a very effective learning experience. Players will benefit by observing their performance, on an individual basis and as a team, during practice and game competition.

# CHAPTER 4

# Ball Collecting (Receiving) Skills

The ability to quickly receive and control passes is essential, particularly at higher levels of competition where players must perform under the pressures of limited space and time. Since passes arrive at various angles and heights, players must learn to collect the ball with different body surfaces, including the feet, thigh, chest, and head. Regardless of the body surface used, however, several basic guidelines should be followed.

• *Move to the ball* — Players must move toward the ball as they are preparing to receive it. Otherwise an alert opponent may cut in front of the receiving player to intercept the pass.

• *Align body with oncoming ball* — The receiving player should position in direct line with the flight of the ball. Correct positioning of the body will shield the ball and ensure that the opponent will not be able to win possession.

• *Provide a soft target* — As the ball arrives the receiving player must cushion the impact by withdrawing the appropriate body surface. Failure to provide a soft target will result in the ball bouncing away, out of the player's range of control.

• *Do not "trap" the ball* — A common mistake is bringing the ball to a complete stop. The needless stopping and subsequent restarting of the ball require extra moments which can prove crucial at advanced levels of play. Players will benefit if, while receiving the ball, they push it in the direction of their next movement. In doing so they will gain precious time and space in which to operate.

• *Use body feints* — The receiving player can unbalance the marking defender by using body feints. Deceptive movements serve to create additional space in which to receive the pass.

• *Receive into space away from opponent* — Players must constantly be aware of the position of the defender. The ball should always be received into the space away from the opponent. Proper shielding technique will ensure that the receiving player maintains ball possession.

# TECHNIQUES FOR COLLECTING GROUND PASSES

## Inside of the Foot

The inside portion of the foot, often used for short range passing, is also an effective surface for receiving and controlling passes.

*Receiving with the inside of the foot.*

### METHOD OF SKILL EXECUTION

1. *The ankle* of the receiving foot is firm with toes pointed up and away from the midline of the body. Provide a large surface with which to collect the ball.
2. *The receiving foot* reaches out to meet the ball as it arrives.
3. *The leg* is withdrawn as the ball contacts the foot, taking the pace off the pass.

### COMMON PROBLEMS / ADVICE

PROBLEM:   Ball bounces away, out of range of control.

ADVICE: Provide a "soft" receiving surface. Cushion the ball as it contacts the foot.

PROBLEM: Ball pops into air.
ADVICE: Contact the ball along its horizontal midline. Contact on the lower half will result in the ball popping upward.

## Outside of the Foot

The outside portion of the instep can be used to receive a pass while tightly marked. The player must position his body between the oncoming ball and the opponent.

*Receiving with the outside of the foot.*

### METHOD OF SKILL EXECUTION

1. *The receiving foot* is firm with toes pointed inward toward the midline of the body.
2. *Position the body* so as to create space between the ball and opponent.

3. *Cushion the ball* as it contacts the outer surface of the instep.
4. *Turn the ball* into space away from the defender.

### COMMON PROBLEMS / ADVICE

PROBLEM:   Ball rolls over the foot when attempting to receive and control.
ADVICE:   Be certain that the foot contacts the center of the ball. Contact is made on the large outer surface of the instep.

PROBLEM:   Defending player reaches through and kicks ball away.
ADVICE:   Receiving player must position his body so as to protect the ball from the defender. The pass should be received with the foot farthest away from the opponent.

## Sole of the Foot

The sole of the foot can be us used to receive a ball rolling directly at a player. It is a very basic method of control, and is usually observed in game situations where a player is not under immediate pressure of an opponent. Players who have mastered the technique of rolling the ball with the sole of the foot can use quick changes of direction as an effective means of maintaining ball possession in crowded spaces (i.e., opponent's goal area).

### METHOD OF SKILL EXECUTION

1. *The receiving foot* is elevated slightly off the ground and extended upward.
2. *The balance leg* is flexed for added stability.
3. *The ball* is cushioned between the sole of the foot and the ground.

### COMMON PROBLEMS / ADVICE

PROBLEM:   Ball rolls under receiving foot.
ADVICE: The toes of the receiving foot must be extended upward but the heel should be close to the ground, preventing the ball from rolling completely under the foot.

*Receiving with the sole of the foot.*

PROBLEM:   Feeling of awkwardness in receiving the ball.
ADVICE:   The balance leg must be flexed and relaxed. Otherwise, the player will be unable to quickly readjust to any slight change of direction of the ball.

PROBLEM:   Opponent dislodges the ball from the receiving player.
ADVICE:   Create space between the ball and opponent. The receiving foot must be extended forward as the player's body shields the ball.

# TECHNIQUES FOR COLLECTING LOFTED PASSES

## Instep

The instep portion of the foot can be used to collect air balls that are dropping at a player's feet. This technique is most appropriate when the receiving player is not under immediate pressure of an opponent.

*Collecting the ball with the instep.*

### METHOD OF SKILL EXECUTION

1. *The receiving foot* is elevated off the ground in preparation to receive and control. The foot is extended and the ankle firm.
2. *The balance leg* is slightly flexed at the knee for added stability.
3. *The receiving leg* is released downward at the moment of impact, softly dropping the ball to the ground.

### COMMON PROBLEMS / ADVICE

PROBLEM:    Ball glances sideways off of foot, out of control.

ADVICE: The ball must be contacted on the center of the instep (shoelaces).

PROBLEM: Upon contact with the instep the ball bounces upward rather than dropping directly to the ground.
ADVICE: Prepare to receive by elevating the foot as the ball is descending, prior to contact. At the moment of contact the foot should release downward.

PROBLEM: Ball spins off instep into the player's body. This usually occurs when the receiving foot is pointed upward as the ball arrives.
ADVICE: The receiving foot must be extended, parallel to the ground, at the moment of contact.

## Inside of the Foot

When a pass arrives at approximately knee level, the inside of the foot provides an effective surface for receiving and controlling the ball. The player should face the approaching ball, positioning slightly to the side of the direct line of flight.

### METHOD OF SKILL EXECUTION

1. *The receiving foot* is firmly positioned with toes pointed up and away from the midline of the body.
2. *The receiving leg* is raised and pulled to the side. The angle of flexion at the knee should be approximately 90 degrees.
3. *The leg* is withdrawn backwards as the ball contacts the inside of the foot.

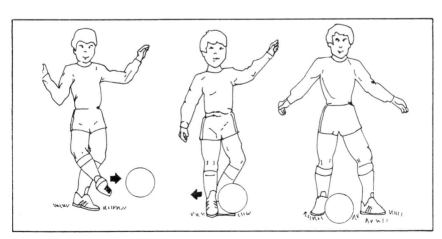

Collecting an air ball with the inside of the foot.

29

# COMMON PROBLEMS / ADVICE

PROBLEM:    Ball rolls over the instep and out of control.
ADVICE:    The inside surface of the foot must contact the ball directly through its center. Contact below the midline will result in the ball rolling over the foot.

PROBLEM:    Ball bounces away from the receiving player, in the direction from which it came.
ADVICE:    Prepare to receive the ball in advance of its arrival. The leg should be elevated early and then withdrawn at the moment of contact. Lack of correct preparation results in poor receiving technique.

PROBLEM:    General feeling of awkwardness in receiving the ball.
ADVICE:    The receiving leg should be flexed and relaxed as the ball arrives. Slight flexion of the balance leg also provides added stability.

## Thigh

The mid-thigh area is often used for controlling an air ball that is dropping from above. The receiving player should position directly beneath the descending ball.

### METHOD OF SKILL EXECUTION

1. *The thigh* of the receiving leg is raised to a position parallel with the ground.
2. *The ball* contacts the mid-portion of the thigh.

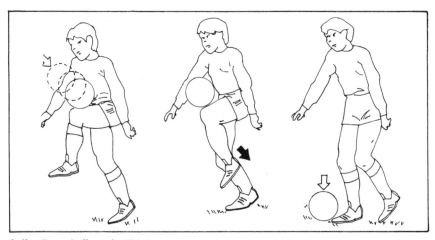

*Collecting a ball on the thigh.*

3. *At the momemt of impact* the thigh is released downward, dropping the ball to the player's feet.

## COMMON PROBLEMS / ADVICE

PROBLEM:   Ball bounces upward, out of control, upon contact with thigh.
ADVICE:   The correct receiving surface is the mid-portion of the thigh where soft tissue aids in cushioning the ball. Contacting the ball too far forward (near the knee) is undesirable. The thigh must be withdrawn at the moment of contact with the ball.

PROBLEM:   Feeling of imbalance and awkwardness when preparing to receive the ball.
ADVICE:   Slight flexion of the balance leg will improve stability.

# Chest

The chest provides an ideal body surface for use in receiving and controlling high lofted balls. The technique is also very effective for shielding the ball from an opponent.

*Arch the upper trunk when receiving the ball on the chest.*

## METHOD OF SKILL EXECUTION

1. *The player positions* between the oncoming ball and opponent.
2. *The upper body* (trunk) is arched backward when preparing to receive.
3. *The ball* contacts the chest slightly to the left or right of center.
4. *Withdraw the upper body* to cushion the impact. (The ball may also be directed past an opponent by a quick turn of the chest.)

## COMMON PROBLEMS / ADVICE

PROBLEM:    Ball bounces upward and over the receiving player.
ADVICE:    The upper body (trunk) must not angle too far backward; otherwise, the ball will skip off the chest.

PROBLEM:    Ball rebounds off chest in the direction from which it came.
ADVICE:    The upper body must be relaxed as the ball contacts the chest.

## Head

Most players think only of heading a ball away, whether it be scoring a goal, passing to a teammate, or clearing a ball from their goal area. However, the forehead can also be used to receive and control a ball descending from above. This is a difficult technique to master, and is appropriate for use only if the receiving player is not under immediate pressure of an opponent.

*Receiving the ball with the head.*

# METHOD OF SKILL EXECUTION

1. *The player* jumps early in order to receive the ball. He should be descending to earth as the ball arrives.
2. *The ball* is contacted on the flat surface of the forehead.
3. *The head* is withdrawn at the moment of impact.
4. *Proper timing* results in the ball dropping at the player's feet.

## COMMON PROBLEMS / ADVICE

PROBLEM:   Ball rebounds upward, out of control.
ADVICE:   The player has probably jumped too late, and as a result has contacted the ball while his body was moving upward. Proper timing of the jump is essential.

### Practice Hints
• Become adept at receiving and *controlling* the ball with either foot.
• *Relax* the body surface contacting the ball to create a cushioning effect.
• Practice receiving and controlling *passes* under the pressures of movement, restricted space, and opponents.
• *Control passes* in one fluid motion. Whenever possible, do not stop the ball dead; rather, receive into space away from the opponent.
• *Concentrate* on watching the ball as it arrives.
• Practice *receiving* balls that arrive from various heights and angles.

### Exercises to Improve Receiving Techniques
• Individual players, each with a ball, *kick the ball* upwards and then practice receiving and controlling the ball as it descends to the ground.
• Position 10-15 yards from a partner. *Pass ground balls* to one another, receiving and controlling with various surfaces of the foot — inside, outside, instep, or sole.
• *Partners,* positioned 20-25 yards apart, chip lofted passes to one another while jogging over various sections of the field. Players must receive and control with thigh, chest, or head.
• *Five players* (servers), each with a ball, form a circle around a teammate. Servers alternate tossing lofted passes to teammate in middle who receives the ball, controlls it, and returns it to server. Drill continues for 1 - 2 minutes, then player in middle becomes a server and one of the servers becomes a receiver.

• *Three players* position in a line. The end players, each with a ball, position ten yards from the player in the center. On command from the coach one of the end players serves a pass to the central player who receives, controls, and returns the ball to the server. The central player then immediately turns to receive a pass from the other end player. The drill continues for 1-2 minutes, after which one of the end players rotates to the central position to receive and control.

• *Three players vs three players* play a game of keep away (ball possession) in an area 20 × 25 yards. The objective for each team is to see how many consecutive passes they can complete before losing possession to the opposing players. The emphasis is on receiving the ball when under pressure of an opponent.

• Organize *small sided games* (5 vs 5, 6 vs 6) which emphasize ball control. For instance, rather than having standard scoring rules, a goal would result whenever a team completes 15 passes in succession. Passing as well as receiving techniques can be emphasized.

# CHAPTER 5

# Passing Skills

Of all the techniques common to the game of soccer, passing skills are probably used with the greatest frequency. Eleven players share one ball, the thread which transforms individuals into a team. In order to achieve cohesive team play each player must develop proficiency in performing the various types of passes. Of equal importance is the knowledge of how to correctly apply those skills in match situations. Inaccurate passing is the swiftest, surest method of destroying the vital teamwork necessary for successful play.

A combination of factors contribute in determining one's level of passing competence. The following guidelines apply to all passing techniques.

• *Watch the ball* — At the moment of contact the player's head should be positioned downward with vision focused on the point of impact.

• *Proper pace* — The velocity of the pass will vary according to the situation. In some cases the ball should be played firmly, while in other instances a softer, more delicate pass, may be appropriate.

• *Proper timing of release* — Players are required to make split second judgements concerning the timing for RELEASE OF THE PASS. Passes initiated too soon lack deception and allow defending players time to readjust their position in relation to the movement of the ball. The player who holds the ball too long limits his available passing options, increasing the likelihood of error. Through practice and game experience players must learn to analyze game situations as they develop and react accordingly.

• *Play positive* — Whenever possible, the ball should be played forward. The penetrating pass creates problems for the defending team. When no positive passing options are available, the ball can be played backward to a supporting teammate as a means of setting up the penetrating pass.

## Inside of the Foot Pass

The inside of the foot pass is a fundamental method of accurately passing the ball over distances up to 15 yards. Although somewhat predictable and lacking deception, it is the skill most commonly used for short range interpassing.

*Inside of the foot pass.*

### METHOD OF SKILL EXECUTION

1. *The ankle* of the kicking foot is firmly positioned with the toes pointing up and away from the midline of the body.
2. *The nonkicking (balance) foot* is planted beside the ball and pointed towards the intended target.
3. *Head* is positioned downward with body over the ball.
4. *The ball* is contacted through its center.
5. *Follow through* with a fluid motion of the kicking leg.

### COMMON PROBLEMS / ADVICE

PROBLEM:   Pass lacks sufficient pace.
ADVICE:   The ankle of the kicking foot must be firm as contact is made with the ball.

PROBLEM:   Ball pops into air rather than rolling along the ground.
ADVICE:   Contact the ball through its horizontal midline. Contact below the center results in a lofted pass.

PROBLEM:   Poor balance.
ADVICE:   The nonkicking foot must be properly positioned.

PROBLEM:   Inaccurate passing.
ADVICE:   The balance foot should be pointed in the intended direction of the pass, with shoulders square to the target.

PROBLEM:   Poor timing.
ADVICE:   The follow-through action of the kicking leg consists of a single fluid motion. At the moment the pass is initiated the player's body should be positioned over the ball.

## Side of the Foot Volley Pass

A bouncing ball, or an air ball that arrives at approximately knee height, can be passed first-time using the side volley. The basic mechanics are somewhat similar to those used with the inside of the foot pass.

The side volley pass.

### METHOD OF SKILL EXECUTION

1. *Face the oncoming ball* and position to the side of its path of flight.
2. *As the ball arrives* the kicking leg is raised and pulled to the side, with a 90 degree angle of flexion at the knee.
3. *The ankle* of the kicking foot is firmly positioned with the toes pointing up and away from the midline of the body.
4. *The balance leg* is slightly flexed at the knee, with the foot pointed towards the oncoming ball.
5. *The ball* is struck directly through its center with a short, sharp follow through of the leg (below the knee).

PROBLEM:   The pass lofts upward in a high arc.
ADVICE:  The kicking foot should contact the ball directly through its center.

PROBLEM:   Inaccurate passing.
ADVICE:   The ankle of the kicking foot must be firm when contacting the ball. Also, the player should prepare to pass by raising the kicking leg into the passing position an instant before the ball arrives.

PROBLEM:   Pass lacks sufficient pace.
ADVICE:   The follow-through motion should be short but powerful.

## Outside of the Foot Pass

The outside portion of the instep is also used in passing the ball. This technique adds deception to short range passing and is an effective means of swerving passes over longer distances.

### METHOD OF SKILL EXECUTION

1. *The kicking foot* is extended down and slightly inward.
2. *The nonkicking (balance) foot* is planted slightly behind and to the side of the ball, and pointed in the direction that the player is facing.
3. *Head* is positioned downward with vision focused on the ball.
4. *To swerve from left to right,* the ball is struck left of center (for a right footed kick) with the outside area of the instep.
5. *Follow through* with an inside-out motion of the kicking leg, initiating movement from behind the balance foot.

### COMMON PROBLEMS / ADVICE

PROBLEM:   Too much spin is imparted to the ball, creating difficulty in controlling the pass.
ADVICE:   Contact the ball with the large outer portion of the instep, not the side of the foot.

PROBLEM:   Poor balance, and a general feeling of awkwardness, in approaching the ball.
ADVICE:   Be certain that the nonkicking foot is pointed in the

*Passing with the outside of the foot.*

direction the player is facing, not in the direction that the pass will be traveling.

PROBLEM:   Inaccurate passing.
ADVICE:   The kicking foot must be firmly positioned at the moment of contact with the ball.

PROBLEM:   Inability to swerve passes over long distances.
ADVICE:   The action of the kicking leg must be a sweeping, follow-through motion, traveling along an inside-out arc.


## Instep Pass

When match situations dictate the need for a long firmly driven pass, the instep of the foot is used to propel the ball. The

*Proper form for the instep pass.*

instep is the area covered by the laces of the shoe. Depending on the placement of the balance foot, the instep pass can either be lofted or played along the ground. Generally, it is suggested that the pass travel along the ground since it can be more easily received by a teammate.

## METHOD OF SKILL EXECUTION

1. *The kicking foot* is held firm and extended downward.
2. *The nonkicking (balance) foot* is placed to the side of the ball.
3. *Vision* is focused on the point of contact with the knee of the kicking leg aligned over the ball.
4. *The ball* is struck directly through its center. (In order to swerve the pass from right to left, the ball is contacted right of center with the inside portion of the instep).
5. *A complete follow-through* will generate power and distance to the driven pass.

## COMMON PROBLEMS / ADVICE

PROBLEM:   The pass fails to travel along the ground (air ball).
ADVICE:   Position the balance foot beside the ball, not behind it,

40

with the kicking foot extended and pointed downward at the moment of contact.

PROBLEM: The pass lacks accuracy and power due to the spinning motion of the ball.
ADVICE: The instep must contact the ball directly through its center axis, minimizing the spin imparted to the pass.

PROBLEM: The ball does not roll smoothly toward its intended target; rather, it bounces along the ground.
ADVICE: Contact the ball with as much foot surface area as possible. The toes of the kicking foot must sweep along the ground, with the large area of the instep impacting the ball.

## Chip Passes

The chip pass is used to loft the ball over an opponent who is positioned between the passing player and a teammate. Two basic techniques are commonly used.

### METHOD OF SKILL EXECUTION

**Short chip pass.**
1. *Kicking foot* is partially extended with the ankle firm.
2. *Nonkicking (balance) foot* is planted directly beside the ball.
3. *Approach* is from behind the ball. The toes of the kicking foot are wedged under the ball with a short, powerful motion of the leg.
4. *Player's body* is positioned over the ball, with the head down, at the moment of contract.
5. There is little or no *follow-through* to the kicking motion.

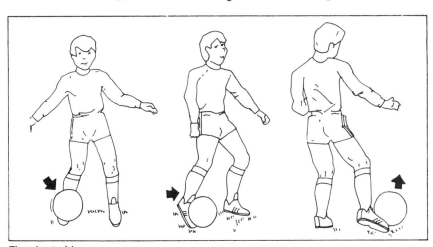

*The short chip pass.*

## COMMON PROBLEMS / ADVICE

PROBLEM:   The pass does not achieve sufficient height to clear the opponent.
ADVICE:   The action of the kicking leg should be short but explosive, wedging the foot underneath the ball.

PROBLEM:   Inaccurate passing.
ADVICE:   May be the result of the nonkicking (balance) foot being placed too far to the side of the ball. It should be positioned at a comfortable distance, usually 8-12 inches.

### Long Chip Pass
1. *Kicking foot* is fully extended and angled slightly inward.
2. *Nonkicking (balance) foot* is planted behind and to the side of the ball.

*Correct technique for the long chip pass.*

3. *Approach* to the ball is from a slight angle. The lower portion of the instep (area of the foot directly behind the toes) is driven through the lower half of the ball.
4. A *complete follow-through* motion is required to generate height and distance to the pass.

## COMMON PROBLEMS / ADVICE

PROBLEM:   Inaccurate passing.
ADVICE:   The kicking foot must be firmly positioned as the instep contacts the ball.

PROBLEM:   The pass is driven rather than lofted, making it difficult for a teammate to receive and control.
ADVICE:   The foot must contact the lower half of the ball, imparting a slight backspin. Providing backspin makes for a "softer" pass.

PROBLEM:   Pass lacks sufficient distance.
ADVICE:   The nonkicking (balance) foot must be placed to the side and behind the ball, allowing for complete follow through action of the kicking leg.

### Practice Hints
• Players must *challenge* themselves during training, continually attempting to reach higher standards of passing excellence.
• Beginners should initially *practice* with a stationary ball, then progress to a moving ball as skill level improves.
• Experienced players should practice *passing skills* under the game related pressures of movement, restricted space, fatigue, and an opponent.
• Regardless of the type of pass, the *kicking foot* must be firmly positioned when contacting the ball.
• *Vision* is always focused on the ball at the moment of contact.
• Players must be equally adept at *passing* with either foot.
• *Passing exercises* should emphasize correct pace as well as accuracy of the pass.

### Exercises to Improve Passing Technique
• *Stationary interpassing* with a teammate over varying distances.
• One- and two-*touch passing* with a partner while jogging slowly.
• *Side-volley* a series of lofted balls to both stationary and moving targets.
• *Short chip passes* over the head of one teammate to the feet of another.

- *Long chip passes* into the space in front of a moving teammate.
- *Two lines of players* are positioned 15-20 yards apart. The first player in line #1 passes to the first player in line #2, then sprints to the end of line #2. Player receiving the ball (in line #2) then passes to the next player in line #1, and sprints to the end of line #1. Repeat for several minutes, first using two-touch passes and progressing to one-touch passes.
- *Three players,* approximately 10-15 yards apart, form a triangle. Player with the ball passes to the teammate of his choice and sprints to that position. Player receiving the ball passes to the third person in the triangle and sprints to that position. Drill continues for several minutes of continuous passing and interchanging of positions.
- *Passing-possession game.* Two teams, each consisting of 8-10 players, play a keep-away game in one half of the field area. A goal is scored when a team manages to complete ten passes in succession, without the opponents intercepting the ball.

# CHAPTER 6

# Dribbling and Shielding Skills

The one versus one confrontations which often occur require that players develop dribbling and shielding skills. Mastery of these techniques is essential for maintaining possession of the ball in crowded conditions.

## Dribbling

Dribbling is a very individualistic skill. The correct technique is not easily described since players may use different methods of beating an opponent. Although general guidelines apply to all dribbling skills, creative players will use variations of the basic movements to express themselves in different ways. What works for one might not suit the style of another. Regardless of individual differences, however, the objective remains the same — maintaining ball possession while taking on and beating an opponent. Intelligent use of dribbling skills at opportune times can destroy a defense. However, players must realize that dribbling is effective only if used at opportune times. Excessive dribbling disrupts team play and usually results in loss of possession. The tactical aspects of when and where to dribble will be discussed in a later chapter (Principles of Attack).

### Dribbling in Restricted Space

The ball usually attracts a crowd. As a consequence one must be able to dribble under conditions where opponents limit the space available to maneuver with the ball. In those situations a miscue generally results in loss of possession.

### METHOD OF SKILL EXECUTION

1. Assume a *slightly crouched* position for greater stability and body control.
2. *The ball* is kept under close control at all times.
3. *The head is up,* as much as possible, enabling one to recognize available passing options.

*Dribbling in confined space.*

4. *Use body* feints to unbalance the marking defender.
5. *Use quick changes* of speed and direction to accelerate past opponents.

## COMMON PROBLEMS / ADVICE

PROBLEM: Player fails to recognize pressure from opponent and loses possession of the ball.

ADVICE: Do not constantly look at the ball while dribbling. Although it is necessary to focus vision on the ball at the moment of contact, the head should be up at other times so that the player is aware of the immediate surroundings.

### Dribbling into Open Space

Players will sometimes find themselves in possession of the ball with open space to the front. In those situations the individual can create problems for the opposition by dribbling at maximum speed toward the defense. Penetrating runs with the ball will force opposing players to readjust their positions, and may create open space between and behind defenders which can be exploited by the attacking team.

It is essential that the player be able to dribble at top speed. Any delays will provide opponents time to recover goal-side to thwart the attack. In order to maximize dribbling speed in the open field, players should follow several basic guidelines.

*Dribbing at speed in open space.*

## METHOD OF SKILL EXECUTION

1. Using the inside or outside surface of the *instep,* push the ball ahead into space and sprint to it. Then push it again.
2. While *striding* to the ball the body is held erect, not crouched as when dribbling in a crowd of players.
3. Keep the *head up* as much as possible; maintain good field vision.
4. On a *breakaway* choose the most direct route to goal.

### COMMON PROBLEMS / ADVICE

PROBLEM: Player experiences difficulty running at top speed while in possession of the ball.
ADVICE: The ball should be pushed ahead so the player can stride out and sprint. Unlike the technique used when dribbling in restricted space, where the ball is kept under close control with short choppy steps, the running stride is lengthened when dribbling in open areas.

## Shielding

Each player must learn the technique for maintaining possession of the ball when tightly marked. The ability to shield, or screen, depends upon correct positioning of the body in relation to the ball and the pressurizing defender.

### METHOD OF SKILL EXECUTION

1. *Position* between the opponent and the ball.
2. *Control* the ball with the foot farthest from the pressurizing player. For instance, if an opponent approaches from the left side, the ball should be controlled with the right foot.
3. Use *quick changes* of direction to unbalance the opponent.
4. Use *body feints* (dip of the shoulder, quick turn of the head, etc.) to create deception.
5. Quickly *re-position* in response to the movement of the pressurizing defender. Maintain sufficient space between the ball and opponent.

### COMMON PROBLEMS / ADVICE

PROBLEM: Defending player reaches through and pokes the ball away.

*Position the body to shield the ball.*

ADVICE: Increase the distance between the ball and opponent. The player in possession should assume a slightly crouched position with a wide base of support (feet apart).


**Practice Hints — Dribbling and Shielding**
• Keep your *head up;* look down only when contacting the ball.
• *Be deceptive;* change speed and direction.
• Develop the ability to *dribble and shield* the ball with either foot.
• Practice *feinting movements* to create space between yourself and the opponent.

*Use feinting movements when dribbling to unbalance the defender.*

### Exercises to Improve Dribbling Technique
• *Run* with the ball, nudging it along with various surfaces (inside, instep, and outside) of the foot.
• *Partners,* each with a ball, play follow the leader. One partner dribbles while the other attempts to closely follow. On a command from the coach the players reverse positions.
• Set up a *series of cones,* positioned 3-4 yards apart. Dribble in and out of the cones at maximum speed while keeping the ball under close control.

• *Dribbling* relay race. Players dribble at maximum speed over a distance of 30-40 yards before exchanging the ball with a team-mate.

• *Dribble* among a crowd of teammates in a restricted area (i.e., center circle), maintaining close possession of the ball while avoiding other players.

• Practice various body *feints* while taking on a defender and moving toward goal.

• Each player *dribbles* at a leisurely pace in a designated area of the field. On repeated commands from the coach the players practice quick changes of speed and direction while maintaining possession of the ball.

**Exercises to Improve Shielding Technique**

• *Shield* the ball from a teammate who attempts to gain posses-sion in a restricted area (10 yards by 10 yards).

• *Receive a pass* while tightly marked by an opponent. Shield the ball until a support player arrives.

• Place *10-15 players,* each with a ball, within the center circle. All players dribble and shield their ball while attempting to kick opponent's ball out of the area.

# CHAPTER 7

# Heading Skills

Soccer is the only major team sport in which the head is used to propel the ball. Heading skills are used for passing to teammates, for defensive clearances, and for scoring goals. It is a complex technique, requiring coordinated movement as well as precise timing.

**Offensive Heading.**

Although the skills appear quite similar, offensive (attacking) heading differs from defensive heading it its basic objectives. Offensive heading is used for two primary purposes; either passing to a teammate or striking on goal. As with other passing techniques, accuracy of service is extremely important. The ball should be passed to a teammate's feet where it can be more easily controlled. When attempting to score, the ball should be driven on a downward angle toward the goal line, preferably to a corner away from the goalkeeper. It is much more difficult for the keeper to handle low shots than those arriving at waist height or above. Deflection headers, which suddenly change the flight path of the ball, are also effective for creating scoring chances in the goal area.

**Defensive Heading.**

Defending players must develop the ability to outleap opponents to clear lofted balls from the area in front of their goal. Correct technique requires that three basic guidelines be followed. First, the ball must be headed high into the air, providing defending teammates an opportunity to reorganize. Second, the ball should be cleared as far as possible from the goal area. Third, the ball should be directed wide toward the touchline, preferably to a teammate. Defenders should follow this basic rule of thumb when clearing a ball — head it high, far, and wide.

## METHOD OF SKILL EXECUTION

1. *Face the oncoming ball* with body positioned in direct line with the path of flight.

*Defenders must be able to win the air ball.*

2. *Watch the ball.* Vision is focused on the point of impact.
3. *Leap straight upward,* attempting to contact the ball at the highest point of the jump.
4. In preparing to strike the ball the *upper trunk* is arched back, with neck rigid and chin tucked in toward chest.
5. The ball is contacted on the flat surface of the *FOREHEAD.*
6. *Attack the ball.* At the moment of impact the upper trunk is snapped forward. Proper timing of the snaplike body motion provides power to the head-driven ball.

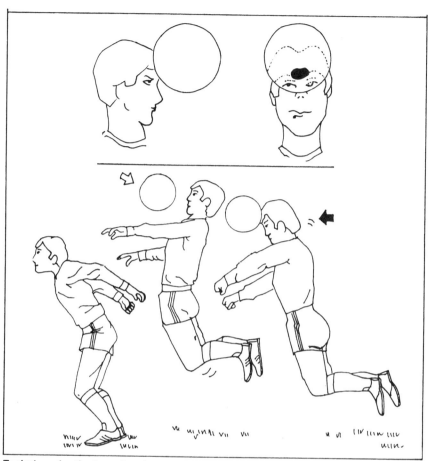

*Technique for the jump header.*

## COMMON PROBLEMS / ADVICE

PROBLEM:   The ball pops straight upward upon contact with the head.
ADVICE:   The ball should be contacted on the forehead just above the eyebrows. Contact on the upper forehead, near the hairline, will result in the ball traveling upward. This technique may be appropriate for defensive clearances but not for passing or scoring goals.

PROBLEM:   The head-driven ball lacks power and velocity.
ADVICE:   The upper trunk and head should not snap forward until the moment of contact. Improper timing diminishes velocity imparted to the ball.

PROBLEM: Player lacks accuracy in passing the ball.
ADVICE: For maximum control the ball should be contacted on the flat surface of the forehead. Contact with the side, top, or back portion of the head should occur only when attempting deflection headers.

PROBLEM: Player mis-times the vertical jump and misses the high lofted ball.
ADVICE: Watch the ball and judge its trajectory before moving into position to head.

### Diving Header

The diving header is an exciting and acrobatic technique which can be effective for scoring off low crosses in the goal area. Likewise, defenders can also use the diving header to clear low driven balls. Players should exhibit caution in performing this technique, however, since an opposing player may at the same instant attempt to kick the low ball. The diving header should be used only when there are no opponents in the immediate area.

## METHOD OF SKILL EXECUTION

1. *Dive toward* the oncoming ball, with body extended and parallel to the ground.
2. *The head* is tilted back with vision focused on the point of contact.
3. *The ball* is contacted on the forehead.
4. *The arms* are extended forward and angled down to cushion the fall.

## COMMON PROBLEMS / ADVICE

PROBLEM: Ball skips off top of the head and continues past player.
ADVICE: The ball must contact the area of the forehead directly above the eyebrows. Contact on the hairline, or on top of the head, will result in the ball traveling upward or behind the player.

### Practice Hints
• Keep the eyes open and *vision* focused on the ball as it arrives.
• Keep the *mouth closed* to avoid biting the tongue.
• Initial skill development should begin from a *kneeling position*. Coordinate the snaplike motion of the upper body which provides power to the driven ball. Once correct body movement is achieved, progress to a standing position.

*The diving header.*

- Practice proper takeoff to achieve the highest *vertical leap.*
- Don't wait for the ball to strike the forehead; *snap forward* to meet it.
- *Timing of the jump* is critical. Attempt to takeoff early and hang in the air, contacting the ball at the highest point of the leap.
- Gradually progress to *heading exercises* which involve a greater degree of difficulty, the ultimate pressure being that of an opposing player.


**Exercises to Improve Heading Technique**
- *Partners,* standing 5 yards apart, alternate tossing lofted balls to one another. Each toss is headed back to the server.
- Slowly jog forward while *heading* a ball served by a teammate. Repeat jogging backward.
- Player (A) positions approximately 8 yards front and center of the goal. Servers (B & C), positioned near each goal post, alternate *serving* balls *into the goal* area for player A to head on goal. Drill continues for one minute, then players rotate positions.
- Servers position on the flank areas of the field and drive high cross *passes into the goal* area. Central player attempts to score off crosses, heading the ball downward to a corner of the goal.
- Playing as a defender, player practices *clearance headers* to a target as teammates serve lofted crosses into the penalty area. (An opponent may also be positioned in the penalty area to provide added pressure on the defender clearing the ball.)
- Practice scoring goals off the *diving header* as a partner serves low crosses.

# CHAPTER 8

# Tackling Skills

Tackling skills are defensive techniques used to dislodge the ball from an opponent. Ideally, the defending player should attempt to strip the ball, gain possession, and initiate an attack. However, as a measure of last resort, it is sometimes necessary to merely kick the ball free to thwart a dangerous scoring attempt or to provide defending teammates time to reorganize.

There are three basic types of tackles. The block tackle is the preferred technique since it is considered a "constructive" form of tackling. That is, the defending player attempts not only to dispossess the opponent of the ball but also to win possession. Two other types, the poke and slide tackle, are "destructive" techniques designed only to set the ball free.

## Block Tackle

The block tackle has several advantages over other techniques. It provides the greatest degree of body control and enables the individual to recover should the initial tackle be unsuccessful. Also, once the ball has been won, the tackling player is in a position to quickly counterattack.

Players should prepare to tackle by following a few basic guidelines. First, they must assume a proper defensive posture. The knees are slightly flexed, lowering the center of gravity, and a staggered stance employed with feet a comfortable distance apart. The distance maintained between the defender and attacker can vary depending upon the abilities of both players. In general, the defending player positions far enough away so that the attacker cannot accelerate past him with the ball, but near enough to apply immediate pressure should the opponent make a mistake. The defender should attempt to delay the attacker while maneuvering into position for the tackle. At the opportune moment he must quickly close the distance and win possession of the ball. Discipline, patience and timing are essential in order that the block tackle be successful.

*The block tackle.*

## METHOD OF SKILL EXECUTION

1. *Approach* the opponent in possession of the ball from the front.
2. Assume a slightly crouched *stance.*
3. *Watch* the ball.
4. At the correct moment *block* the ball with the inside surface of the foot. The ankle must be firm.

## COMMON PROBLEMS / ADVICE

PROBLEM:  Defending player fails to win the tackle and is unable to quickly recover.
ADVICE:  Maximum body control is required for the successful tackle. The defender must crouch and maintain a good defensive stance. Upon deciding to tackle, do so with great power and determination. A halfhearted attempt is worse than no attempt at all.

PROBLEM:  Defending player constantly overcommits when closing to tackle and is easily beaten.
ADVICE:  Maneuver to delay the opponent before attempting the tackle. The defending player must "set-up" the attacker to maximize the chances of winning the ball.

## Poke and Slide Tackles

Poke and slide tackles are also effective means for freeing the ball from an opponent. However, these techniques are not designed to win possession but merely to prevent development of the opponent's attacking play. They are appropriate only when the block tackle is not possible.

As the term implies, the poke tackle requires that the defender kick the ball away from the attacker with his toe. The technique can be effectively used when an opponent is shielding

*The poke tackle.*

the ball, or when the defender has been beaten on the dribble. In either case the defender reaches in, usually from the side, and pokes the ball loose.

The slide tackle should be used only as a last resort, in situations when a player is clearly beaten and has little hope of catching the opponent. The technique requires the defender to slide into the ball in an attempt to kick it free. It is essential that the tackler first contact the ball, not the opponent, in order to avoid a rule infraction. A major drawback of the slide tackle is that, if the ball is not freed from the opponent's possession, the defender is left with little chance of recovery.

*Defender (in black) has missed the slide tackle and is beaten.*

### Practice Hints
• Learn to judge the *proper distance* in positioning so as not to be beaten on the dribble.
• Maintain good defensive *posture* and body control.
• Use *body feints* to entice the attacker into revealing his intentions.

- *Do not commit yourself* to the opponent's deceptive movements. Watch the ball at all times.
- *Timing* of the tackle is crucial for success. Practice quickly closing the distance to the opponent when tackling.

**Exercises to Improve Tackling Technique**
- *Partners* practice blocking the ball from each other, concentrating on the correct technique and proper timing of the tackle.
- *One versus one* dribbling/tackling game. One player attempts to dribble past a teammate to a designated line. The teammate attempts to tackle the ball. If the dribbler beats the defender to the line he is awarded one point. If the defender executes a successful tackle he is awarded two points. The game continues until one player accumulates 20 points, then they switch positions.
- *Ten players,* each with a ball, dribble in an area 10 by 10 yards. Two defenders enter the area and attempt to win the ball from the dribblers. If a defender tackles and gains possession, two points are awarded. If he pokes a ball away from any dribbler, but does not win possession, he is awarded one point. Game continues for 3-4 minutes, with the defender accumulating the most points declared the winner. Repeat game with different defenders.

# CHAPTER 9

# Shooting Skills

The ultimate aim of every attack is to finish with a score. Each player, regardless of position, must develop the ability to shoot with power and accuracy using either foot. Although several types of shots are commonly used, a few basic guidelines are applicable to all. If followed, these rules will aid in improving one's shooting ability.

• **Watch the Ball** — At the moment of contact the head should be held steady with vision focused on the point of impact.

• **Kicking Foot Extended** — The kicking foot should be extended downward and held firm when striking the ball.

• **Quick Release** — The ability to instantly get off a shot when presented with an opportunity is of the utmost importance. He who hesitates does not score many goals.

• **Nonkicking Foot** — The balance leg should be planted to the side of the ball, not behind it. Correct placement aligns the body over the ball and aids in achieving the desired low shot. Planting the foot behind the ball forces the player to lean backwards and increases the likelihood that the shot will rise over the goal.

• **Follow-through** — A smooth, complete follow-through motion will provide power and accuracy to the driven ball.

The choice of shooting technique depends upon whether the ball is rolling, bouncing, or arriving through the air. Coaches can prepare their players by using a variety of drills during practice sessions. Whenever possible, shooting exercises should be conducted under simulated game conditions which include the pressures of restricted space and time, fatigue, and an opponent.

## Instep Drive

The most commonly used technique for striking a stationary or a rolling ball is the instep drive.

### METHOD OF SKILL EXECUTION

1. The *kicking foot* is extended and held firm with toes pointed down.

*The instep drive.*

2. The *nonkicking foot* is planted beside the ball and pointed toward the intended target.

3. The *shoulders* are positioned square with the target.

4. The *instep* surface of the foot (laces) contacts the center of the ball.

### COMMON PROBLEMS / ADVICE

PROBLEM: Shot has a spinning motion and fails to achieve sufficient power.

ADVICE: The foot must contact the vertical center of the ball. Striking the ball on either side of center will impart spin and reduce velocity of the shot.

PROBLEM: The shot fails to stay low and travels over the goal.

ADVICE: A high shot is usually due to the player leaning back when striking the ball. It is essential that the body be aligned over the ball at the moment of contact. Proper positioning of the balance leg (beside the ball) and the kicking foot (extended down) will aid in achieving a low trajectory on the driven ball.

PROBLEM: Inaccurate shooting.
ADVICE: When possible, align the shoulders square with the intended target. If the shoulders are angled away from the target, it is likely that the shot will be pulled in that direction.

## Front Volley

Players must develop the ability to shoot without first setting up the ball. A bouncing ball, or an air ball, can be struck first-time using the volley shot.

### METHOD OF SKILL EXECUTION

1. *Position* in direct line with the flight of the oncoming ball.
2. The *balance leg* is slightly flexed to provide maximum stability.
3. The *kicking foot* is extended down at the moment of contact.
4. The *knee* of the kicking leg is positioned over the ball as it is struck.
5. *Kick down* through the ball with a short, powerful motion of the lower leg.

*The front volley shot.*

# Side Volley

First-time shooting of an airborne ball dropping to the player's side is a difficult technique to master. The most important consideration is to keep the shot low.

## METHOD OF SKILL EXECUTION

1. The *kicking leg* is raised horizontal to the ground and in line with the flight of the ball. When possible, the knee should be at a higher level than the ball.
2. The top half of the ball is struck with the *instep* surface of the foot.
3. Attempt to kick on a *downward angle* through the ball.

*The side volley shot.*

## COMMON PROBLEMS / ADVICE

PROBLEM:   Shot travels in a high arc over the goal.
ADVICE:   With both the front and side volley, it is very important that the knee be positioned over the ball at the moment of contact. Proper positioning will ensure a low trajectory on the shot.

# Half Volley

The half volley shot results when a ball dropping from the air is struck just as it contacts the ground. Precise timing is essential since contacting the ball even a fraction of a second late results in an inaccurate shot. When properly executed, tremendous power and velocity can be generated from the half volley.

### METHOD OF SKILL EXECUTION

1. *Position* in direct line with the flight of the descending ball.
2. *Strike through* the center of the ball as it contacts the ground.
3. The *kicking foot* is extended down with knee over the ball.
4. The *nonkicking foot* is planted directly beside the ball at the moment of contact.

# Swerving "Banana" Shot

It is sometimes advantageous if the ball does not travel in a straight line toward goal. Shots which curve in flight are appropriately termed "banana" shots. A curved trajectory can be achieved by applying proper spin to the ball. Bending or swerved shots, particularly from free kick situations, can be very effective since they create difficulty for the goalkeeper in correctly judging the flight of the ball.

### METHOD OF SKILL EXECUTION
(for a right footed kick)

1. The *kicking foot* is extended down and held firm.
2. To *curve a shot* from right to left, contact the ball right of

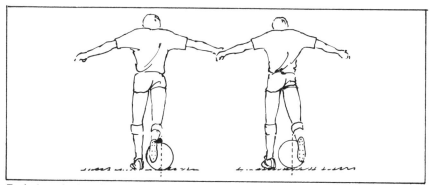

*Technique for bending or swerving shots.*

center with the inside portion of the instep. The kicking motion will impart a counterclockwise rotation to the ball.

3. To *curve a shot* from left to right, contact the ball left of center with the outside portion of the instep. The kicking motion will impart clockwise rotation to the ball.

4. A complete follow-through motion will produce *maximum spin* and result in greater curve in the flight of the ball.

(***Reverse the technique for a left footed kick)

### COMMON PROBLEMS / ADVICE

PROBLEM: Ball fails to curve during flight.
ADVICE: Usually results from failure to impart sufficient spin. The instep must contact either the right or left half of the ball. Striking through the central portion will not generate the spin required to curve the trajectory of flight.

PROBLEM: The shot lacks power and velocity.
ADVICE: The ball must be contacted slightly left or right of center, but not too far along its outer perimeter. It is important to contact the ball with as much foot surface area as possible in order to achieve maximum control and power.

## Bicycle Kick

The most acrobatic of all shots is the bicycle kick. The technique derives its name from the scissor-like motion of the legs, and is used when attempting to shoot a ball that is traveling overhead. The player must leap, throwing his legs upward and over his head, and with a bicycle-like motion strike the ball. The correct form looks quite similar to peddling a bike upside down.

Players should use the bicycle kick with caution. If performed incorrectly serious injury may result. As the kicker descends to the ground he must use his arms and hands to break the fall. Otherwise he may end up landing on his head, neck or upper back. When practicing the bicycle kick it is suggested that players work in pairs. A partner can aid in cushioning the fall until the correct technique is developed.

### Practice Hints
• *Practice* the various shooting techniques using both feet.
• *Develop* the ability to shoot first-time.
• *Concentrate* on accuracy over power.

• Use *shooting exercises* which simulate actual game conditions (pressures of limited time, restricted space, and opponent)
• *Aim shots* low and toward the corners of the goal; these are the most difficult for a goalkeeper to save.
• *Practice* long range shooting (outside the penalty area) for midfielders and defenders.

**Exercises to Improve Shooting Technique**
• *Shoot* stationary balls placed at various spots in and around the penalty area.
• *Partners* (A & B) position 30 yards from goal. Player A serves a rolling ball past player B who turns, sprints to the ball, and takes a first-time shot. Partners alternate taking shots.
• *Partners* (A & B) position 25 yards from goal. Player A, with the ball, faces the goal while player B positions with his back to the goal. Player A tosses a high lob over the head of player B who turns, sprints to the bouncing ball, and volleys or half volleys on goal. Players alternate turns shooting.
• Player *passes* to a teammate, receives a return pass (give and go), and shoots at goal.
• Each player, with a ball, positions 40 yards from goal. On command from the coach each player *dribbles* at top speed towards goal and shoots. (Increased pressure can be applied on the shooter by adding a chasing defender to the drill.)
• Control long, cross *passes* from a teammate and shoot on goal.
• *Two* players *vs two* players in the penalty area. The objective of the drill is for each team (two players) to score as many goals as possible. The coach begins the exercise by serving a ball into the area. The team gaining possession of the ball attempts to score while the other team defends. When a shot has been taken, or the ball kicked out of the penalty area, the coach immediately serves another ball to continue play. If the defending team steals the ball they can immediately shoot to score. The game continues until one team has scored five goals.
• Practice *free kick* situations by bending or curving stationary balls around an obstacle into the goal.

# CHAPTER 10

# Positional Responsibilities

Soccer, above all things, is a team game. Success or failure ultimately depends upon whether eleven individuals can mesh into a smoothly functioning unit. Philosophies of team play are constantly changing, however, as coaches search for the ideal method of accomplishing that aim. In the not so distant past positional responsibilities were far more restricted than today. Fullbacks were regarded strictly as defenders, assigned the duty of protecting their goal. Forwards were given the responsibility of scoring goals, and were not expected to have more than a passive interest in the team's defensive scheme. Midfielders, as always, carried the bulk of the workload, being required to support both the attack and the defense with equal vigor. Due to the rigid team structure and limitations imposed upon players, the general run of play was often quite predictable. Imagination and innovation were lacking.

All this has changed, however, with the continued evolution of the sport. The modern game stresses total involvement of

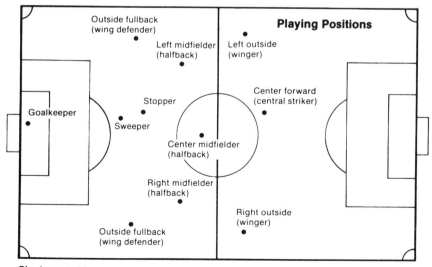

*Playing positions.*

all players, including the goalkeeper, with tactical concepts based upon constant movement and frequent interchanging of positions. For the most part, coaches must be concerned with developing "total soccer players", individuals who can successfully make the transition from attack to defense, and vice versa.

Although positional play is becoming less specialized within the framework of the team, each position still has basic attributes associated with it. In selecting which player to place in what role, the coach should take into account the strengths of the individual and attempt to match them with the responsibilities required of the position.

## Goalkeeper

The goalkeeper remains the one true specialist on the soccer team. He is, in reality, the last defender — the final barrier that opposing teams must conquer in order to score — and is assigned the difficult task of protecting a goal 24 feet wide and 8 feet high. In defense of the goal the keeper is permitted to use his hands in controlling the ball, and as a consequence must perform an entirely different set of skills than do the field players. The position is a demanding one, both physically and mentally, and it takes a special type of athlete to accept the challenge.

Although goalkeepers come in all shapes and sizes, several basic attributes are characteristic of top flight netminders.

## PHYSICAL ATTRIBUTES

### Size

Since the soccer goal is 8 feet high, and the keeper is often required to field high, lofted passes dropping into the goal area, a tall individual may have a decided advantage over a shorter person. However, many factors interact to determine one's ability as a goalkeeper. Individual's can compensate for a lack of height through proper timing and correct positional play.

### Hands

The goalkeeper must be skilled at catching and holding the ball. Shots arrive from various angles, traveling at different velocities, and the keeper must field them cleanly to avoid giving up rebounds or dropped balls in the goal area.

*The goalkeeper is the only player permitted use of the hands in controlling the ball.*

### Quickness

The ability to instantly react, whether it be to a powerful drive from outside the penalty area or a close-in deflected shot, is essential. Top-class netminders possess catlike quickness which enables them to adjust to sudden changes in the flight of the ball.

### Strength

The ball always attracts a crowd when played into the goal area, so the keeper must be prepared for a strong physical challenge from opponents. Development of upper body strength will aid the goalkeeper in meeting the challenge.

# MENTAL ATTRIBUTES

### Concentration
The goalkeeper must devote full attention to the game at all times. This is a difficult task, especially in matches where the keeper rarely touches the ball. One mistake can cost the game, however, and the keeper must always be ready to come up the game winning save when needed.

### Anticipation
The ability to anticipate the movements and intentions of opponents will enable the keeper to position to best advantage. It is a talent which occurs naturally for some, but for many it is acquired only through diligent study of opponents and actual game experience.

### Courage
The goalkeeper position is not for the timid. The roughest physical action usually occurs in the vacinity of the goal, with the keeper sometimes involved in jarring collisions. He must have the courage to dominate the goal area, whether it be challenging an attacker for a crossing pass or blocking the point-blank shot of a goal-hungry forward.

## Defenders
Virtually all great teams are based on a strong, technically sound defense. Although every field player has a role in the team's defensive efforts, the defenders, or fullbacks, assume the bulk of the responsibility. Most modern formations consist of a four-man fullback line, employing two central defenders flanked by right and left wing defenders. One of the central defenders is usually designated as the sweeper, or libero, who supports the other three fullbacks. The other central defender, designated as the stopper back, typically marks the opposing center forward or striker. The wing defenders are usually responsible for marking the opposing wingmen. The sweeper, freed from the responsibility of man-to-man marking, functions as the "extra" defender by providing cover for the stopper and wing defenders. Present day tactics also require that defenders contribute to the team's attacking efforts. No longer can a player be only one dimensional — he must be competent offensively as well as defensively.

All great defenders seem to possess certain qualities that allow them to excel above others. If a young player can combine these attributes with a sound technical knowledge of defensive concepts, they will be well on their way to becoming a fine defender.

### Tenacity
Defending players must possess a mental and physical make-up which drives them towards perfection. They cannot become easily discouraged, and must doggedly persevere in attempting to neutralize the attacking efforts of opponents. Determination will often help make up for physical limitations.

### Strength in the Air
Defenders, particularly those occupying central positions, must be a dominant force in the air. The ability to outjump opponents and win air balls is a virtual necessity, since defending players are constantly challenged for passes lofted into their goal area.

*Defenders must outjump opponents to win air balls.*

When heading to clear, a basic rule should be followed — direct the ball high, far, and wide. If possible, the clearance should be headed away from the central area in front of the goal to a teammate who is in position to initiate a counterattack. The ball should never be headed downward in the area of the defender's own goal.

### Tackling Skills

The act of challenging an opponent in possession of the ball is termed tackling. This is a very important skill, yet it is often neglected in training sessions. Since the art of tackling is a primary method of regaining possession of the ball, every player must work hard to develop the proper technique.

Tackles should be made clean and hard with determination to win the ball. When the decision to tackle has been made, the player must act without hesitation. Half-hearted attempts, typically the result of indecision or a lack of confidence, invariably leave the defender beaten and unable to recover.

### Game Sense

Quality defenders possess the uncanny ability to read situations as they develop and respond accordingly. They always seem to be in position to intercept passes or break up an attack. It is not mere luck that top-flight defenders analyze the play so well; rather, it is usually the result of serious study of the game coupled with actual playing experience. A high skill level does not guarantee that one will become a top defender. Skill must be accompanied by tactical awareness, intelligence, and over-all game sense.

## Midfielders

Midfielders provide the vital link between the attack and defense. They are expected to operate effectively over an area ranging from deep in their own defensive zone to the opponent's goal area. They cover a great deal of territory and must be able to perform under heavy physical strain. Research indicates that, in a typical game, a midfielder usually runs a distance of more than five miles.

The success or failure of a team depends ultimately on the performance of it's midfield players. Since most attacking maneuvers originate in the middle sector of the field, as do the initial lines of defense, midfielders must be adept at the transition game. They are responsible for establishing the tempo and style

*Midfielders play a vital role in the team's attack.*

of play. Modern systems required that midfielders assume an integral role in the attack. When the opportunity arises they must move forward into attacking roles to place added pressure on opposing defenses.

Many of the top international teams are built around great midfield players, individuals who can dominate play at both ends of the field. These world class athletes possess certain qualities which enable them to perform at a high standard of play.

### Fitness

Although every soccer player should be highly conditioned, midfield players are usually required to run longer and harder than their teammates. They must be at peak physical condition to successfully carry out their responsibilities. Players who are not physically fit soon discover that performance diminishes markedly as fatigue begins to erode their ability to execute the necessary skill movements. Although fitness is not everything to a soccer player, it provides a foundation upon which all other aspects of the game are based.

### Composure

Midfielders serve as field generals for the team. They must conduct themselves with confidence and composure in pressure situations. Whether it be in the first or final minutes of a game, the emphasis should always be for consistency of performance.

### Creativity

In order to exploit the weaknesses of opposing defenses, it is essential that midfield players possess good field vision. They must be creative and innovative in their movements, always looking to change the point of attack to their team's best advantage. Predictability of play is to be avoided.

## Forwards — Strikers and Wingers

One of the greatest thrills in soccer is scoring an important goal. Young players throughout the world dream of that special moment when they will become the hero — the ball smashing against the back of the net, the roar of the crowd, the congratulations of teammates. A goal scoring forward does receive a fair share of adulation, and rightly so. With the improved sophistication of modern defensive systems, the forward who can score or create goals with relative consistency is a very important commodity.

Although terminology  may vary with the system of play, individuals who occupy the front-running, attacking positions are generally classified as either strikers or wingmen. The wingmen operate in the flank areas of the field and are responsible for providing width to the attack. Through calculated movement and their ability to penetrate opposing defenses, wing forwards create open space and scoring opportunities for their teammates. They also function to initiate many attacks by withdrawing into their own half of the field to receive outlet passes from defensemen or the goalkeeper. Defensively, wingers usually mark the opposing wing fullbacks should they make overlapping runs.

The center forward, or central striker, spearheads the attack and is usually considered the team's primary goal scorer. Since the striker is tightly marked, he must be an opportunist at creating goals out of half chances and defensive mistakes. He must be able to perform skillfully in pressure situations under the restrictions of limited time and space. Although primarily an attacking player, the striker also has defensive responsibilities. He must challenge for possession of the ball in the central, attacking third of the field, and prevent opposing defensemen from moving forward, unmarked, to aid in their team's attacking efforts.

It is difficult to pinpoint the reasons why one player develops into a dominant forward while another, with equal physical ability, never quite achieves full potential. The great attackers possess the physical and emotional make-up that enables them to succeed at their profession while others with equal talent fail. The following qualities are important factors influencing successful attacking play.

## Mobility

Players must be mentally willing and physically able to work hard when not in possession of the ball. They must constantly strive to create space for themselves and teammates through intelligent running patterns, runs designed to draw opponents into poor defensive positions. Such movement, termed "off the ball running", is vital for the overall success of a team's attacking efforts.

## Strength on the Ball

The ability to control the ball when under pressure of an opponent is essential. While receiving the pass a player must maintain possession, even though tightly marked, and be prepared for the hard knocks which invariably occur.

*Forwards must be opportunistic, creating goals out of half chances and defensive errors.*

## Shooting Ability

The ball always seems to attract a crowd, especially in the goal areas. As a result, forwards must be able to quickly release their shot in a variety of situations. First-time shooting, the ability to shoot without setting up the ball, is essential. Quick decisions and subsequent reactions in pressure situations result in goals, just as indecisive movements lead to failure. In addition to a quick release, forwards must possess the ability to shoot equally well with both feet. Many a scoring opportunity has been wasted because the ball was first played to the stronger foot before the shot was attempted. In order to become a complete soccer player, and to score goals at high levels of competition, players must develop shooting competence in either foot.

## Determination and Confidence

Physical skills alone do not ensure that one will enjoy success as a forward. Attitude and emotional make-up are often the deciding factors in distinguishing great players from average ones. Determination to succeed, and the ability to bounce back and overcome adversity, are essential mental attributes. It is difficult for the coach to instill such qualities in a player; they are usually self-motivated and originate from within.

Confidence also plays a deciding role in determining whether an individual reaches his full potential. This is not to imply that a player be arrogant or underestimate the opponent. True confidence involves a realistic appraisal of one's abilities, allowing for maximal functioning of physical and mental skills under match conditions.

It is important to realize that, although forwards generally receive the greatest acclaim, a score is usually the result of total team effort. Everyone has a role in the process — the goal-keeper who initiates the attack with accurate distribution, defenders who push forward in supporting roles, midfielders who link the defense with the attack, and players who draw opponents out of position to create opportunities for teammates.

A goal scored, regardless of who tallies, is the ultimate purpose of team efforts. Players must accept the challenge and seize the opportunity. However, they cannot be selfish and expect to contribute significantly to the overall team effort. If the opportunity to shoot doesn't materialize, don't force the situation. Rather, the ball should be played to a teammate in a better position to finish the play.

# CHAPTER 11

# Principles of Attack

Scoring remains the most difficult task in soccer. The challenge has become even greater in recent years with the onset of newer and more sophisticated defensive schemes. In order for a team to generate a potent attack, players must combine skill and determination with intelligent tactical play.

Whereas skill performance involves executing such precise physical movements as passing or heading, tactics deal primarily with decision-making. During the course of a game players are required to make split-second choices from a variety of alternative behaviors. For example, decisions must be made concerning the type of pass to use in a given situation, where and when to dribble, whether to shoot or pass, and where to position to best advantage when not in possession of the ball. Individuals who consistently make the wrong decisions, even though physically talented, will prove a detriment to the team's attacking efforts.

Several basic concepts underlie the organization needed to create a successful attacking system. Knowledge of these principles will enhance one's tactical awareness and serve as a guideline for decision-making.

## 1. Width and Depth in Attack

The playing field is quite large, usually exceeding the dimensions of the typical American football field. The attacking team must use all available space to their advantage. A primary objective is to create and then exploit space in the scoring areas. By spreading the attack from touchline to touchline opposing players will be drawn into the flank areas, creating gaps within the defense.

Providing depth, or support, in the attack is of equal importance. It is essential that the player in possession of the ball be presented with several passing options. Teammates should assume support positions to the rear, to the side, and in advance of the ball. Proper support allows for effective passing combinations and aids in maintaining ball possession.

## 2. Player Movement (without the ball)

Two teams (22 players) must share one ball. Research has demonstrated that each player has possession for only three to four minutes during a 90 minute game. For the remaining 80 odd minutes players must work hard without the ball to constructively add to the team's attack. Much of their efforts should be devoted to creating space for both themselves and teammates through off-the-ball running patterns.

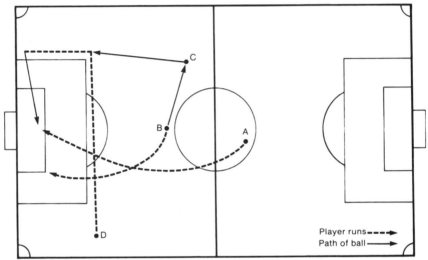

*Tactical running patterns. Server A plays the ball to target B who passes to support player C. C passes the ball into the open space on the wing area. Player D makes a cross-field run and collects the ball, dribbles to the endline, and crosses the ball to the near post. Player B has made a run to the far post while the original server A has run to the near post.*

• **Diagonal Runs** — The nature of a player's run is very important. The most direct route to goal is not always the optimal choice since the marking defender will also end up in a central position favorable to the defense. Runs should be designed for the dual purpose of penetrating the defense while at the same time drawing opponents away from central positions. Diagonal running patterns achieve both aims.

• **Creating Space for the Individual** — It is much easier to perform the necessary skills when given ample time and space in which to operate. Defending players realize this fact, however, and try to limit the space available to opponents by tight marking. Attacking players must counter with a variety of movement patterns in order to free themselves of the marker. Unpredictable movements may cause the defender to hesitate at times, enabling the attacker to break free of coverage. The clever player will "set-up" an

84

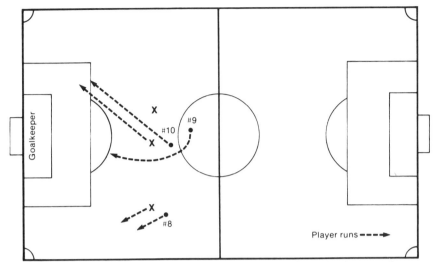

*Diagonal running. Diagonal penetrating run by #10 draws the defender away from the central position and creates space for #9 in a dangerous scoring area. The winger, #8, takes his man away from the play. Diagonal runs serve two purposes: to penetrate the defense and also to draw defenders away from the goal area.*

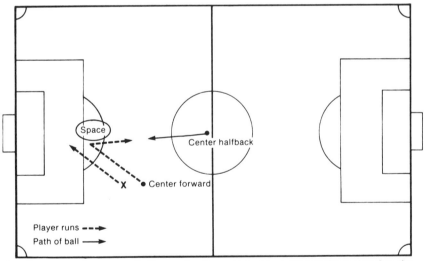

*Creating space for yourself. The center forward makes a diagonal run drawing the defender with him. Suddenly, the forward stops and withdraws, creating the desired space in which he can receive and turn with the pass given by his center halfback.*

opponent by using quick changes of speed and direction. For example, if an attacking player slows his run, the marking defender must also slow down or delay. A quick burst of speed will accelerate the attacker away from the opponent into open space.

Checking runs are also an effective means of creating space for the individual. The attacker must make a convincing attempt to sprint past his marking opponent. At the last moment, however, he stops short of the defender and withdraws toward a teammate about to serve the ball. The unexpected change of direction will usually increase the distance between himself and the marking defender, creating space and time in which the ball can be received and controlled. This tactic is commonly referred to as "checking off" a defender.

• *Creating Space for a Teammate* — Players can also use diagonal running patterns for the specific purpose of creating space for a teammate. For example, a wing forward who makes a diagonal run through the center of the defense draws a defender with him, clearing space on the flank into which a midfielder can advance.

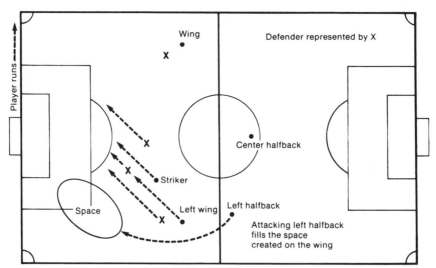

Creating space for a teammate. Left wing forward runs diagonally across the middle of the defense, drawing the wing defender toward the center of the field. Space is created in the wing area vacated by the defender.

## 3. Creative Interpassing

Once the attacking team has created space in which to operate, they must quickly exploit the most vulnerable areas through combination play (interpassing). Since the ball travels faster than a player can run, it is advantageous to use one and two touch passing. Players should look for the penetrating pass when possible, one which by-passes opponents and puts them temporarily out of the play. This is not meant to imply that every pass must be directed forward. Sometimes a square pass (across the field) is necessary to set up the penetration pass. Square passing should be limited, however, since excessive use tends to slow the attack and allows defending opponents time to recover goal-side of the ball.

It is important to frequently shift the point of attack so that play does not become predictable. Diagonal cross passes serve to quickly change the direction of play and force opponents to readjust their positions. Players possessing good field vision will channel the attack into areas of the least resistance (most space and fewest defenders).

### 4. Create a Numerical Superiority

Teams will improve their chances of successfully penetrating opposing defenses if they can consistently generate a numerical advantage of players in a given area. For example, if the attacking team creates a 3 versus 2 situation in a flank area, it is not possible for the two defenders to mark the three attackers. The extra attacker, if used properly, is free to penetrate the defense. This is accomplished through proper support positioning coupled with precise combination passing. The ability to create these small group situations (3 vs 2, 4 vs 2, 4 vs 3) is critical to the overall success of a team's attacking efforts.

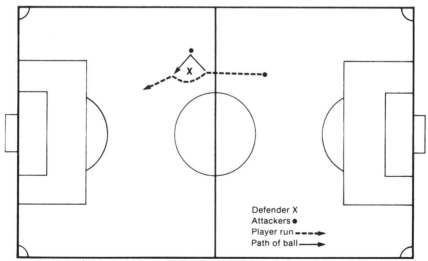

*Running with the ball; the give and go pass. When dribbling the ball, go directly at your opponent until he commits to you. At that moment, pass to your teammate and sprint to open space for a return pass.*

87

## 5. Utilize Space Behind the Defense

Defenders are coached to keep the play in front of them. Inexperienced players will sometimes carry this point to an extreme, becoming so overly concerned with the position of the ball that they neglect to protect the space behind them. This fault is often referred to as "ball watching." An attacking team can take advantage of a ball watching defender by drawing him forward and then playing the ball into open space behind the defense. A well-timed run coupled with an accurate through pass may free a teammate for a strike on goal.

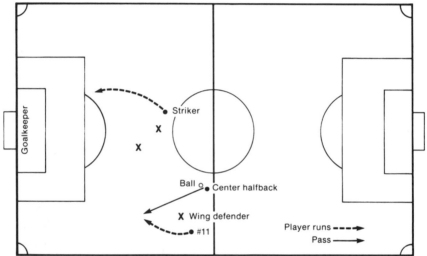

*Utilizing space behind the defense. A penetrating pass directed into space behind the wing defender X frees the wing forward #11 for a strike at goal. Proper timing of the pass and run is crucial for success.*

## 6. Dribbling (at opportune times)

Excessive dribbling often leads to the demise of a team's attacking efforts. However, when used in appropriate situations, dribbling skills can be very effective in increasing a team's goal scoring productivity. Players, and more importantly the team, will benefit from following a few basic guidelines with regard to where and when to dribble.

It is tactically sound to limit the incidence of dribbling in the defensive third of the field, an area where one mistake may result in an opponent's score. Defending players, when in the vicinity of their own goal, should never attempt to dribble by an opponent. Rather, they should pass the ball to teammates in more forward positions, or play the ball back to their goalkeeper. Since defending players have the responsibility of quickly initiating the attack, they should concentrate on playing one and two-touch soccer whenever possible.

Dribbling may occur more frequently in the central portions of the field but still should be used sparingly. It is the responsibility of midfield players to smoothly mesh the defense with the attack. Excessive dribbling increases the risk of possession loss and leads to a sluggish and often predictable style of play. Successful midfield play is characterized by quick movement of the ball using one and two-touch passing.

Dribbling can be utilized to best advantage in the attacking third of the field. Players with creative dribbling skills should be urged to take on the defender in circumstances where the attacking team has created a 1 vs 1 match-up within striking distance of the goal. Under those conditions an attacker with the ability to beat a defender on the dribble is a valuable asset. Otherwise, even in the attacking third of the field, excessive dribbling should be discouraged. Players must always be willing to give the ball to a teammate occupying a more advantageous scoring position. The selfish "ball hog" hurts not only his own performance but the overall team effort.

*Dribbling skills are most effectively used in the attacking third of the field.*

## 7. Finish the Attack

As evidenced by the relatively few goals scored at higher levels of play, the successful completion of an attack is probably the most difficult task in soccer. Once created, opportunities must not be wasted. Coaches are well aware of that fact, and spend a considerable amount of practice time devoted to the refinement of shooting skills. However, often these exercises do not simulate game conditions where players are required to release shots under limitations of restricted space and time. As a result players do not become accustomed to scoring goals under the actual pressures encountered during play. It is important that coaches design and implement shooting exercises which incorporate such factors as fatigue, first-time shooting, and pressure of an opponent into the drills.

From a tactical point of view, the angle from which a shot is attempted is of critical importance. Shots taken from the flank areas, where the angle to goal is reduced, have little chance of finding the back of the net. Shots attempted from central areas, where the angle to goal is large, have the greatest chance of beating the goalkeeper. Teams will benefit by gearing their attack toward creating scoring opportunities in areas which provide a wide angle to goal.

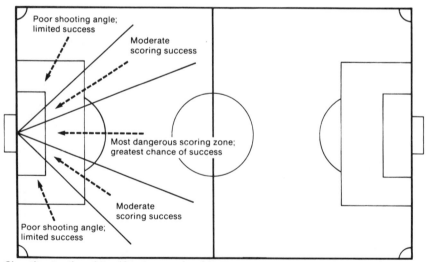

*Shooting tactics. Attacking teams should attempt to create numerous scoring opportunities in the most dangerous scoring zone centrally located in front of the goal.*

## SUMMARY:
### Responsibilities of Attacking Players

- Maintain ball *possession.*
- *Move* to create space for yourself and teammates.
- *Look* for the penetrating (killer) pass.
- Provide *support* for the teammate with the ball.
- Use *creative* dribbling in the attacking third of the field.
- Accept the challenge of finishing *scoring* opportunities.

# CHAPTER 12

# Principles of Defense

It is a misnomer to label players as defenders, midfielders or forwards. In reality, every player becomes a defender when his team loses the ball. Each must contribute in thwarting the opponent's attack and regaining possession. However, organization of a solid defense does not rest on individual play alone. Defensive responsibilities exist on both a personal and team basis. An understanding of the basic principles underlying individual and team defense will enable players to mesh their talents with intelligent tactical play to create a strong defensive side.

## Individual Defense

### 1. Defensive Stance

It is important to maintain good balance and body control. A staggered stance, with feet a comfortable distance apart and one planted slightly behind the other, is used when defending in a 1 vs 1 situation. Correct posture ensures maximum mobility, enabling one to readjust to the quick movements of an opponent.

### 2. Defensive Positioning

Defending players should follow two basic guidelines when positioning to mark an opponent.
• *Position Goalside* — Position between the opponent and the goal. From that location the defender is able to keep both opponent and ball in vision.
• *Position Inside* — Defending players must take precautions not to get beaten to the inside (center area of field) where a wide shooting angle exists. Position to cut off the inside route to goal.

### 3. Marking Distance

Once positioned, tight coverage must ensue to deny the opponent possession of the ball. The proper covering distance (between defender and attacker) depends upon several factors.

*The defending player positions goalside of his opponent.*

• *Area of the Field* — In the defensive third of the field, within shooting range of the goal, marking must be very tight. As play moves away from the defender's goal area the marking can be looser.

• *Ability of Opponent* — Defending players must take into consideration the speed, quickness and skill of their opponent. An expremely fast attacker who may lack a high degree of skill should be given a little more room to negate the speed advantage. On the other hand, a highly skilled opponent must be marked very tightly so as to deny the time and space needed to utilize those skills to best advantage.

• *Position of the Ball* — The proper covering distance also depends on the location of the ball in relation to the opponent. In general, the more distant the ball the looser the marking. Any opponent in the immediate area of the ball must be tightly marked. Should a long pass be directed to a player being loosely marked, the defender must close the distance between himself and the opponent while the ball is traveling.

*Force the opponent toward the sideline where space is limited.*

## 4. Containment

Once an opponent gains possession the responsibilities of the marking defender change. The following objectives are of primary concern:

• *Prevent* the opponent from *turning* with the ball. If the attacker can turn and face the defender's goal, he will be able to penetrate with the ball or serve passes forward into vital spaces.

• When an opponent *successfully turns* toward goal, the defender must position to prevent the penetration pass while forcing the attacker toward the sideline where space is limited.

• The marking defender should attempt to *delay* the opponent's forward *movement* until teammates are positioned to provide defensive support.

## 5. Win the Ball

Once support (cover) positioning has been established, the marking defender can attempt to tackle at an opportune time in order to win possession.

# Team Defense

Defending players must be effectively organized to collectively limit the space and time allowed opponents. With regard to team defense, two general philosophies have persisted through the years — zonal and man-to-man. Arguments concerning the relative merits of each still provide cause for debate in most soccer circles. It is apparent that each method has certain inherent strengths and weaknesses.

Strict zonal coverage requires each player to be responsible for a specific area. An opponent entering a zone immediately becomes the responsibility of the defender assigned that area. Upon leaving the zone he becomes the responsibility of another defender. An advantage of zonal defense is that correct positional play usually results, as defenders should not be easily drawn away from their respective areas. Critics argue that zonal marking provides opponents too much space in which to operate. The seams between zones are particularly vulnerable since defenders may be hesitant in moving to the perimeter of their area to mark an opponent. Flooding a zone with more than one opponent also causes problems since it puts the defender at a numerical disadvantage.

Man-to-man defense, as the term suggests, requires each defender to mark a specific opponent. A positive aspect of man-to-man coverage is that, in theory, all opposing players are tightly marked. The chance of an opponent running free is less than with zonal marking. However, the man-to-man marking system is not without problems. Inexperienced players may be drawn into poor defensive positions by intelligent off-the-ball running of opponents. In addition, if the attacking team can successfully isolate a great individual player against a less talented defender the marking scheme will breakdown. Finally, some players have difficulty recognizing the proper time to release from their man to contribute in their team's attack. The result is a defensive, unimaginative style of play.

Which system is more effective? Which method should your team use? It is obvious that a combination of both, utilizing the strong points of each, is the optimal choice. Each player must be aware of individual positional responsibilities (zonal) but also realize that an opponent entering a critical area must be tightly marked (man-to-man). As a general guideline, man-to-man marking should be used in the immediate area of the ball with zonal coverage used to protect vital space in areas of the field away from the ball.

96

Regardless of individual philosophical differences which may exist among coaches, several basic principles should be applied to a team's overall defensive scheme.

## 1. Immediate Chase

When a turnover occurs, the player nearest the ball should apply immediate pressure in an attempt to regain possession. If the opponent retains control, however, the defender's responsibility is to delay forward penetration. The opposition must not be allowed to initiate a quick counterattack before the defending team is properly positioned.

## 2. Concentrated Defense

Concentrating defenders in the most dangerous scoring zones has become an accepted standard. While immediate chase is occuring in the vicinity of the ball, the remaining defenders must quickly retreat to a position goalside of their man and the ball. Within their own half of the field, players should locate to protect the most critical defensive space. Since most scoring opportunities originate in central areas which provide the widest shooting angle, defenders must limit the time and space available to opponents in those areas. The tactic of consolidating or compacting the defense achieves that aim.

## 3. Depth in Defense

Defenders should never align flat across the field. As players withdraw to organize in the most vital areas, they must position so that a penetrating pass cannot beat the entire defense. Support positioning is required to protect the space behind individual defenders. Depth in defense is achieved with each player supported by a covering defender.

## 4. Pressuring

Tight coverage of opponents is commonly called pressuring. Depending upon coaching preference, some teams apply pressure in all areas of the field while others pressure only in their defensive half, allowing the opposition to freely advance the ball to the midline. Regardless of which method is used, a basic rule should be followed — the closer an opponent moves toward the defender's goal, the tighter the marking.

*Tight marking of opponents around the goal area is imperative.*

### 5. Goalkeeper as Defender

The goalkeeper provides the last line of support and is responsible for covering the open area behind the fullback line. He must anticipate passes which penetrate that vital space and be prepared to leave his goal to collect the ball. Defenders, when under intense pressure from an opponent, should also consider the option of playing the ball to the keeper as a means of maintaining possession.

### 6. Initiate the Attack

Modern tactics require that a defending player do more than merely disrupt the opponent's attack. Winning possession is only the first step in the process. A smooth transition from defense to attack must follow.

### 7. Contribute to the Attack

Back defenders must move forward in support of front running teammates. A common tactic used to involve these players in the attack is the overlap. As the term implies, the defender makes a curved run from behind a teammate and moves into a more forward position. In order for the overlap to be effective, the area must first be cleared. Diagonal runs by the forwards, from the flank areas toward the center, will draw opponents inward and create open space into which the defender can overlap. Proper timing of the run is critical to its success. If the defender advances too soon the element of surprise will be lost. He must delay until the area is free of opponents and then sprint forward into the open space.

# COACHING HINTS

The principles of both individual and team defense can be taught and reinforced through the use of small group exercises. For example, all of the individual tactics (defensive stance, marking, containment, etc.) can be covered in a 1 vs 1 game situation. Small-sided games (reduced numbers) also serve a useful purpose in practicing the concepts of team defense. Virtually all of the principles can be demonstrated in a 3 vs 1, 3 vs 2, or a 4 vs 3 gamelike situation.

# SUMMARY:
## Responsibilities of Defending Players

* *Position* goalside and inside of your opponent
* Use a staggered *stance* with feet a comfortable distance apart
* Keep the ball and opponent in *vision* at all times
* *Contain* and delay the opponent — do not overcommit
* Position to *prevent* the penetrating pass
* *Force* the opponent into restricted space — use the sideline and endline as teammates
* Use the *goalkeeper* as a support player
* *Initiate* the counterattack

99

CHAPTER **13**

# Restart Situations

Restart (dead-ball) situations, including direct and indirect free kicks, corner kicks, throw-ins, and penalty kicks, provide excellent scoring opportunities. In modern soccer, particularly at the higher levels of play, a majority of goals (over 50%) originate from restarts. Coaches should devote a significant portion of the practice time to organizing and perfecting the team's ability to score from, as well as defend against, dead-ball situations.

## ATTACKING FROM SET PIECES

### Free Kicks (Direct and Indirect)

A variety of free kick plays can be used, depending upon the preference and imagination of the coach. Several basic guidelines should be followed for the development of effective set plays.

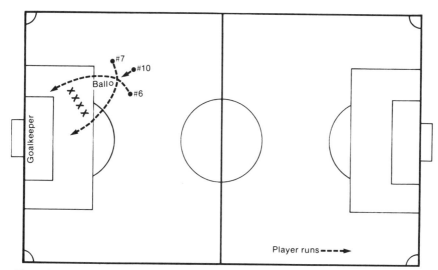

*Direct free kick. Player #6 runs over the ball to the right of the defensive wall, player #7 follows with a run to the left, player #10 then follows with a strike at goal.*

- **Be organized** — Players must have a complete understanding of their individual roles as well as the overall objective of the play.
- **Keep it simple** — The more complicated the play the greater the likelihood of error. Limit the number of passes (ideally two or less) required to create a strike on goal.
- **Involve deception** — Add an element of deception to confuse defenders. This can be accomplished through player movement prior to the kick (i.e., runs over the ball).
- **Create a strike on goal** — A free kick which does not result in a scoring chance must be considered a failure. Regardless of individual variations among free kick plays, the primary objective is to score.

## Corner Kicks

Corner kicks also provide excellent opportunities for goal scoring, particularly for teams who are dominant in the air. Two basic types of corner kick plays are commonly used.

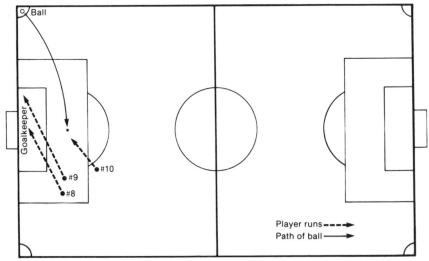

*Corner kick. Timed runs are made by three attacking players, #8, #9, and #10. Players #8 and #9 run to create space in front of the goal for #10 to fill. Player #10 must delay his run until space has been vacated by #8 and #9.*

The far-post serve attacks the space located at either the center or far-post area of the goalmouth. The kick is usually lofted to a spot 8-12 yards front of the goal, where the goalkeeper will have difficulty leaving his line to collect the ball. Through the use of patterned runs, the attacking team attempts to free a player in the open space to head the ball home.

The near-post corner has gained popularity in recent years. Rather than serving the ball across the goalmouth, the kick is driven hard and low toward the nearest post where an attacker times his run to meet and deflect the ball on goal. When properly timed, the near post run is very difficult to defend against.

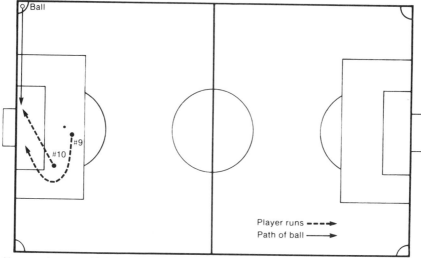

Near post corner kick play. The ball is driven powerfully to the near post where #10 runs to meet and deflect the ball into the goal. Player #9 curls his run to the far post in case the ball sails to that area.

## Throw-In

In the past the throw-in was not considered a direct means for creating scoring opportunities. Its primary function was to return the ball into play after it had passed over the touchline (sideline). That philosophy has changed, however, with the

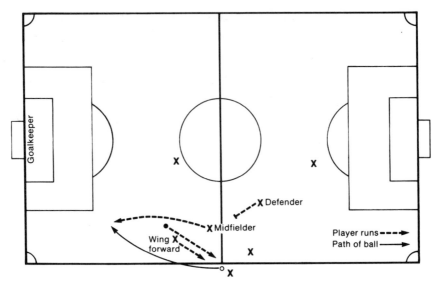

*Throw-in. The wing forward, who is tightly marked, runs toward the thrower. The midfielder runs into the space vacated by the wing forward to receive the throw-in.*

development of the "long throw". Through improved technique and training methods, certain players have acquired the ability to throw the ball over distances of 30 yards or more. This tactic can be particularly effective when restarting play in the opponent's end of the field, where the ball can be tossed directly into the goalmouth. In those situations the long throw can serve the same purpose as a corner kick.

## Penalty Kick

The penalty shot is strictly a one-on-one situation, a result of the defending team committing a direct foul within their penalty area. The ball is placed on a spot 12 yards directly in front of the goal. On the referee's signal it is the kicker versus the goalkeeper.

The following suggestions should be considered when taking a penalty kick.

• *Decide in advance* which corner of the goal to shoot at when the whistle is blown. Most penalty shots are missed due to indecisiveness on the part of the kicker.

• *Keep the shot low* and to the side of the goalkeeper.

• Focus *total concentration* on the ball. Don't be distracted by actions of the keeper or opposing players.

• *Relax!* Strike the ball with confidence.

# DEFENDING AGAINST SET PIECES

## Free Kicks (Direct and Indirect)

Coaches must take great care to ensure their team is prepared to defend against direct and indirect free kicks. Even a moments hesitation in organizing the defense may prove disasterous.

When a free kick is awarded within shooting range of the goal, the defending team should immediately implement the following steps.

### 1. Build a wall.

A line of players (wall) should be placed ten yards from the ball to block the path to goal. The wall is positioned to defend the near post area while the goalkeeper is responsible for any ball played to the far post. The number of players in the wall will vary, depending upon the spot of the foul. As many as five players are used when the ball is located in an area providing a wide shooting angle. Fewer players are included when the ball is spotted in a flank area (narrow angle). The goalkeeper should indicate how many teammates he wants in the wall. However, it is not his responsibility to align the wall since he must be ever watchful should the opponents attempt a quick shot. A field player is usually designated that responsibility.

### 2. Mark opponents.

Opposing players in the vicinity of the goal area must be tightly marked. Loose coverage results in goals against.

### 3. Mark vital space.

Defenders not in the wall should position to prevent opponents from playing the ball into space behind the wall. The inner lanes to goal must be covered.

******* *When the free kick is out of shooting range, formation of a wall is unnecessary. In this instance, defenders should use man-to-man coverage and position goalside of their opponent.*

## Corner Kicks

The basic principles for defending against corner kicks are similar to those used for free kicks. All opponents in the goal area must be tightly marked. Most teams place a defender inside each goal post to protect against shots to that area. The goalkeeper positions in the center portion of the goal, a yard or so off the line. The remaining players have individual man-to-man marking responsibilities. Some coaches, depending upon the availability of players, will also assign one or two defenders zonal coverage in the most critical areas.

## Throw-In

The team should defend against the long throw in the same manner as with corner kicks. Marking must be very tight in the defending third of the field. As the play moves to where the ball cannot be thrown directly into the goal area, coverage can adjust to a combination of zone and man-to-man.

# CHAPTER 14

# Systems

Students of the game are continually searching for the ultimate system of play. The debate over which system is best has not been resolved as evidenced by the changing philosophies over the years. We can expect the game to undergo continued changes in the future since, in reality, the perfect system of play does not exist. It is a popular misconception that systems win games. A variety of factors, ranging from individual physical ability to group tactical preparation, interact to determine team success. The system of play is only one factor to consider among many.

A common mistake made by many coaches is first choosing a system and then forcing players to fit into that formational setup. As a rule of thumb, the system should be selected based upon its ability to maximize strengths and minimize limitations of team members. The capabilities of players must be the deciding factors in matching a specific team with the correct system. Regardless of the system, once the game is underway the organization of players on the field becomes quite similar. Several basic principles are common to all; depth and width in attack, support and concentration in defense, and intelligent tactical movement. Success usually depends upon how well players apply these principles in match competition.

Since a number of systems have enjoyed popularity over the years, a discussion of a few of the more notable ones will provide insight into the changes that have occurred as the modern game evolved. When describing a system, such as the 4-3-3, the first number refers to defending players, the second to midfield players, and the third to attacking players. The numbering includes only the 10 field players.

## 2-3-5 System

During the early years of the 20th century, most teams deployed their players in a formation primarily suited for attacking soccer. The prevalent system was the 2-3-5, with 5 attacking players supported from behind by 3 halfbacks (midfielders),

2 defenders, and of course, the goalkeeper. The attacking players were usually positioned with a center forward, 2 conventional wingers who played wide on the touchlines, and 2 inside forwards. The principal job of the center forward and wingers was to attack, and they were not required to contribute significantly to the defensive efforts of the team. The inside forwards, although also primarily attacking players, withdrew at times to aid their halfbacks in the middle sector of the field.

The halfbacks were saddled with the bulk of the physical work. They had to fill dual roles, both in attack and defense. Defensively, the wing halfbacks marked the opponent's wingmen while the center halfback marked the center forward. The fullbacks were organized in a zonal defense marking the areas usually occupied by the opposing inside forwards. They played in tandem with one diagonally positioned behind the other to create depth in defense.

Although the 2-3-5 system enjoyed widespread use for many years, the system had obvious limitations. Players were restricted in their roles, mobility was limited, and play was generally predictable. This philosophy did not coincide with the modern concept of "total football", in which all players assume attacking and defending responsibilities.

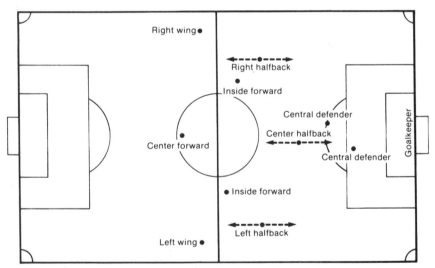

2-3-5 System. The three halfbacks carry the bulk of the workload, supporting on attack and defense. The wing halfbacks function in the same role as wing defenders in the more recent 4-3-3.

## WM System (3-2-5)

Herbert Chapman of FC Arsenal realized the limitations of the 2-3-5 setup and devised a variation of the system. The new formation, known as the WM, was designed to strengthen control of the midfield area. This objective was accomplished with the additional help of the inside forwards, who withdrew into midfield positions and became playmakers as well as goal

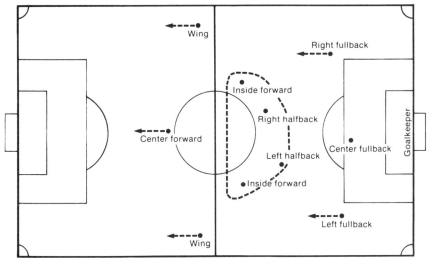

3-2-5 System. The inside forward and halfbacks do the bulk of the running, controlling the midfield areas. With only one central defender, the system is vulnerable at the back.

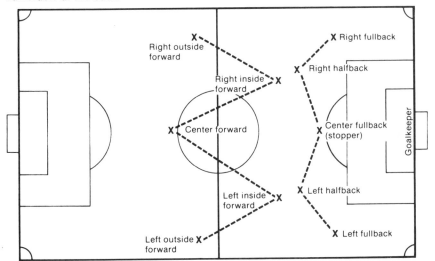

The WM. In this system, the positioning of the players forms the letters WM.

scorers. The center forward remained upfront as a target, spear-heading the attack, as did the wing forwards. The positioning of the 5 attackers resembled the letter W, with 3 frontrunners and 2 withdrawn inside forwards. Two halfbacks positioned in the central area of the field, linking the attackers and defenders, and were given the defensive responsibility of marking the opposing inside forwards. The defenders were organized so that the wing fullbacks marked the opposing wingers and the center fullback marked the center forward. The positioning of the 2 midfielders and 3 defenders resembled the letter M, hence the name WM system.

Although originated through good intent, the WM system had several inherent weaknesses. The strict man-to-man marking required of the back defenders left them vulnerable to intelligent running by opponents; runs aimed at drawing them into poor defensive positions. In addition, since the single central defender was assigned man-to-man marking responsibility, the system lacked adequate defensive support or cover. A covering defender, known today as the sweeper or libero, was nonexistent.

### 4-2-4 System

Oftentimes new and innovative formations first appear at the highest levels of competition. Such was the case in 1958 when Brazil, during the World Cup matches, unveiled the 4-2-4 setup on their way to becoming champions of the soccer world. Blessed with great players such as Pele, Didi, and Garrincha, Brazilian coach Vincente Feola devised a formation that employed 4 defenders, 2 midfielders or linkmen, and 4 attacking forwards. Unlike its predecessors, the system placed greater emphasis on player mobility and interchanging of positions.

The linkmen played a vital role in the 4-2-4 formation. They were required to have excellent positional sense, since two mid-fielders were responsible for covering a large area of the playing field. The midfielders functioned as extra forwards, supporting the front runners, when their team was on the attack. Defensively they usually employed zonal coverage in the central portion of the field. Two central defenders and a right and left fullback occupied the back line of defense. The wing fullbacks, although responsible for marking the opposing wingers, were given the freedom to move forward into the attack when presented with the opportunity. Two central defenders played in tandem, with the sweeper back pro-viding cover for the other defenders. The four front-running attackers consisted of two wingers and two centrally located strikers. These players were not rigidly fixed in position and displayed a great deal of movement both with or without the ball.

The wingmen would sometimes assume a withdrawn position in order to receive outlet passes from the defense, and also to aid the linkmen in control of the flank areas.

The 4-2-4 system introduced a new era in soccer, exemplifying the changing philosophies of play. The emphasis shifted toward the "total player", one who could both attack and defend. Each player was required to understand and accept the responsibilities of a teammate should position switching occur. However, the 4-2-4 was not the last word on systems of play. It was merely a trend setter. There were still improvements to be made and newer methods of play to evolve.

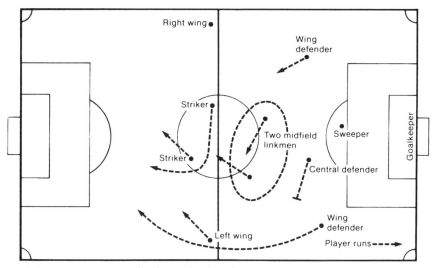

*4-2-4 System. Player mobility is emphasized in this system. The two midfielders function as a link between the attack and the defense.*

## 4-4-2 System

Control of the midfield is vital to the success of every team. Most modern systems are structured around this concept, and are designed to provide maximum coverage of that field area. One such system, the 4-4-2, employs four midfield players. Two central midfielders usually play in tandem, and are flanked on each side by wing halfbacks. One of the central midfielders is usually assigned a defensive role while the other is permitted greater freedom to attack. Two forwards are positioned as dual strikers in the attacking area of the field.

At first glance the 4-4-2 appears to be a defense oriented system, although theoretically it is not. The formation is designed to provide sufficient numbers in both attack and defense. Success of the system depends upon the transition, from defender to attacker, once the ball changes possession. The midfielders, supported by the fullbacks, must quickly move forward into attacking positions to aid the two strikers. If the midfield players do not adequately support the forwards, then the 4-4-2 does indeed assume a defensive character, placing the entire burden of creating goals on the two strikers.

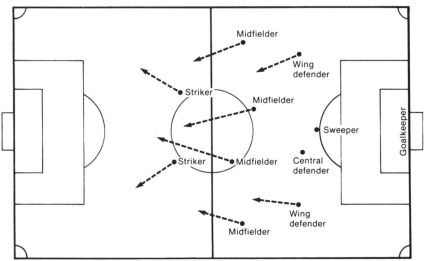

*4-4-2 System. Four players are positioned in the midfield area. On attack the midfielders must assume more forward positions in space created by the front strikers. Wing defenders also move forward in support of the midfield.*

## Catenaccio

Fans and players alike enjoy an attacking, wide-open brand of soccer. However, although pleasing to the eye, such tactics are not always in the team's best interests. Teams that over-attack are extremely vulnerable to swift counterattack from the opposition. At the highest levels of play, where winning is the primary concern, many coaches adopt a very conservative approach to the game.

Several years ago a unique system appeared in the professional leagues of Italy. It arose primarily out of a "fear of losing" philosophy, and quickly gained widespread notoriety. The formation, coined "catenaccio", was designed to pose an impenetrable defense to the opponents. The players were organized as 5 defenders, 3 or 4 midfielders, and 1 or 2 forwards (depending on the coach's personal preference). The system was very successful in accomplishing the desired aim — fewer goals scored (for both teams). However, such tactics made for a boring, unimaginative style of soccer. Many games ended in a 0-0 draw.

Spectators became disgruntled, and many of the players concurred with the sentiments of the fans. Today catenaccio has almost disappeared, a victim of its inability to adapt in accord with the modern philosophy of play.

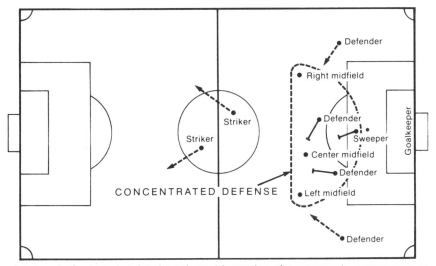

*Catenaccio System. A defensive-oriented formation, the catenaccio system concentrates many players in the dangerous scoring zones. One or two strikers are positioned in forward positions to generate the attack.*

### 4-3-3- System

With greater emphasis placed upon the concept of "total soccer", yet another variation of the 4-2-4 evolved which maximizes player mobility. The 4-3-3 system, as the numbering indicates, positions 4 defenders, 3 midfielders, and 3 forwards. Constant motion is the theme of the 4-3-3. All players must possess offensive and defensive skills, since interchanging of positions is vital if the system is played correctly. The emphasis on mobility allows for the concentration of players in certain areas, a tactic not possible with many of the earlier systems. Groups of players attack as well as defend, providing numerical superiority in a given area of the field.

Tactically, the defenders and midfielders position in their defensive third of the field to deny the opponents critical space. One of the central defenders plays as the sweeper, the free man in defense, and is not assigned man-to-man marking responsibilities. His job is to provide cover for defending teammates. The other central defender, designated as the stopper back, is usually assigned tight marking of the opposing center forward. Wing defenders mark the opposing wingmen.

113

The midfield players, besides aiding in defense, fulfill an important role in the attack. Upon gaining possession of the ball, midfielders must push forward in support of their forwards. Otherwise, the team will find itself outnumbered and at a disadvantage in the opponent's defensive portion of the field. Midfield players undertake more of a goal-scoring role at the higher levels of competition, where the forwards are tightly marked. Intelligent running by the front-runners create open space into which the midfielders can advance for attempts on goal. Overlapping runs by the defenders also add extra players into the attack.

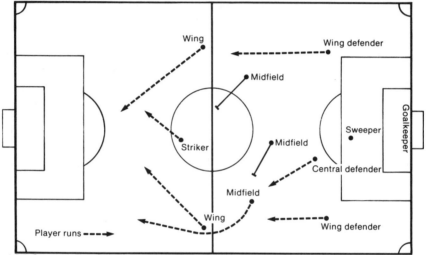

*4-3-3 System. Total soccer is the theme of the 4-3-3 system. All players must possess attacking and defending abilities with midfielders and even defenders moving forward to score goals.*

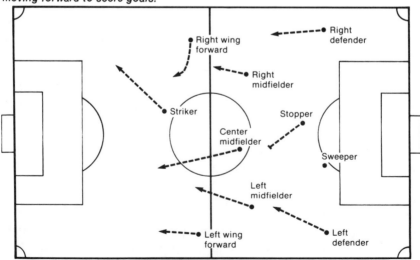

*Movement patterns of the 4-3-3 system. The center striker makes a run to the wing area, creating space for the center midfielder to move forward into an attacking position.*

114

# CHAPTER 15

# Laws of the Game

The laws governing play have been issued by FIFA, the Federation Internationale de Football Association, and apply to all competitions involving teams affiliated with FIFA. It is necessary to have a standard system of laws due to the international nature of the game. Inter-country competition would be seriously hindered if teams located in different parts of the world played under a variety of self-imposed rules.

Within the United States, a few rule variances occur between the different levels of competition (youth, high school, college). Most of these variations deal with the number of substitutes permitted in a match. Otherwise, the laws are generally universal and should be thoroughly understood by coaches and players alike.

The following material is a summarized version of the FIFA Laws.

## Field of Play

The *soccer field* is a large, rectangular playing area. The length may vary from 100 - 130 yards and the width from 50 - 100 yards. International matches limit the length to 110 - 120 yards and the width to 70 - 80 yards. In all cases, the length of the field must exceed its width.

The *area of play* is marked by distinctive lines, not more than 5 inches in width. The side boundaries are called touchlines or sidelines, and the boundaries at the end of the field are called goal lines. The halfway line runs parallel to the goal lines and divides the field into two equal halves.

The *goal area* is a rectangular area at each end of the field of play. Two lines are drawn at right angles to the goal line, 6 yards from each goal post, and extend onto the field of play for a distance of 6 yards. These two lines are joined by a line drawn parallel to the goal line.

The *penalty area* is also a rectangular area at each end of the field of play, with lines drawn at right angles to the goal line 18 yards from each post. These two lines extend 18 yards onto the playing field and are connected by a line drawn parallel to the goal line. The goalkeeper is permitted use of arms and hands to control the ball within the penalty area.

The *penalty spot,* located within the penalty area, is marked 12 yards in front of the midpoint of the goal line. Penalty kicks are taken from this spot.

The *penalty arc* is a line located front-center of the penalty area, having a radius of 10 yards from the penalty spot. All players, except the kicker and goalkeeper, must remain outside of the arc while the kick is being taken.

The *corner area,* marked at each corner of the field, has a radius of 1 yard. When the defending team plays the ball over its own goal line, the opposition is awarded a kick taken from the nearest corner.

The *goals* are positioned on the center of each goal line. The dimensions of the soccer goal are 8 feet high by 8 yards wide.

The *center circle,* with a radius of 10 yards, is drawn in the center of the playing field.

The *center spot,* located on the halfway line, is the midpoint of the center circle. After a goal has been scored and at the beginning of each half of play, the game is restarted by a kickoff from the center spot. Only the team kicking off may position players in the circle prior to the kickoff.

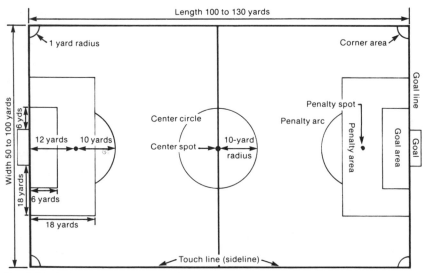

*The field of play.*

## The Ball

An official soccer ball (size #5) is spherical in shape and composed of leather or other approved materials. The circumference can vary from 27 - 28 inches and the weight 14 - 16 ounces. During play, the ball should not be changed unless authorized by the referee.

## The Players

A soccer game is played by two teams, each consisting of eleven players. One of the eleven must be designated as a goalkeeper and is permitted to use his hands within the penalty area. The tactical organization of field players may vary. Several different systems of play are commonly used, and these are constantly changing. The alignment of players on the field is becoming less defined, since modern soccer emphasizes mobility and the ability of players to fulfill both defensive and attacking roles.

## Referee and Linesmen

A soccer game is officiated by a referee assisted by two linesmen. The referee enforces the laws during play and has ultimate authority on the field. The linesmen are positioned on opposite sides of the field. They are responsible for indicating when the ball is out of play and determine which team is entitled to the throw-in, goal kick, or corner kick. The linesmen also aid in signaling offside violations.

## Duration of the Game

The game consists of two equal periods of 45 minutes each. A 5-minute halftime break separates the periods. Youth games may use shorter time periods by mutual agreement.

## Start of Play

A coin toss determines choice of ends and also which team kicks off. The game is started by a player taking a placekick from the center spot into the opponents' half of the field of play. Every player must be in his own half of the field and each member of the opposing team must be at least 10 yards from the ball until it is played. The ball is not considered in play until it travels forward the distance of its circumference, and cannot be played a second time until it has been touched by another player. The game is restarted in the same manner after a goal and also after halftime.

## Ball In and Out of Play

The ball is considered out of play when it has wholly crossed the goal line or touchline, whether on the ground or in the air. At all other times the ball is considered in play, including:
• *Rebounds* from a goalpost, crossbar, or corner flagpost onto the field of play.
• *Rebounds* off either the referee or linesmen when they are in the field of play.
• Until a decision is given for an *infringement* of the rules.
When the linesmen and referee cannot determine who last touched a ball that travels out of bounds, the game is restarted with a drop ball at the spot where the ball was last in play. The referee drops the ball between two opposing players who attempt to gain possession after it has touched the ground.

## Method of Scoring

A goal is scored when the entire ball has crossed over the goal line, between the goalposts and under the crossbar — provided it has not been carried, thrown, or intentionally propelled by the hand or arm of an attacking player. Each goal scored counts for a single point during the course of a match, and the team scoring the most goals is declared the winner. If the game ends with an equal number of goals scored by both teams, it is termed a draw.

## Offside

A player is offside if he is closer to his opponents' goal line than the ball at the moment the ball is played unless:
• He is in his *own half* of the field of play
• Two opponents are nearer to their *own goal* line than he is.
• The ball last *touched an opponent* or was last played by him.
• He *receives the ball directly* from a corner kick, goal kick, throw-in, or when dropped by the referee.
A player in an offside position is not penalized unless, in the judgement of the referee, he is interferring with the play or with an

opponent, or is seeking to gain an advantage by being in an off-side position. Punishment for an infringement of the offside law is an indirect free kick awarded to the opposing team from the spot where the infringement occurred.

Offside is not judged at the moment the player in question receives the ball, but rather at the moment the ball is played by a member of his own team. A player who is not in an offside position at the instant one of his teammates passes the ball toward him does not, therefore, become offside if he goes forward during the flight of the ball.

## Fouls and Misconduct

When a player commits a foul or some other form of misconduct, the opposing team is awarded a free kick as a result of the illegal behavior. A direct free kick is assessed for intentionally:
• *Kicking* or attempting to kick an opponent.
• *Tripping* an opponent.
• *Jumping* at an opponent.
• *Charging* an opponent in a violent or dangerous manner.
• *Charging* from behind unless the opponent is penalized for obstruction.
• *Striking* or attempting to strike an opponent.
• *Holding* an opponent.
• *Pushing* an opponent.
• *Handling* the ball (except for the goalkeeper in his own penalty area).
If a defending player intentionally commits one of these offenses within his own penalty area, a penalty kick is awarded to the opposing team.

*Indirect free kicks are* as a result of the following infractions:
• Playing in a *dangerous manner.*
• *Charging* with the shoulder when the ball is not within playing distance of the players involved; playing the man rather than the ball.
• *Intentional obstruction* of an opponent when not playing the ball.
• *Charging* the goalkeeper except when he is holding the ball, obstructing an opponent, or has passed outside of his goal-area.
• When the *goalkeeper* has taken more than four steps without releasing the ball, or used tactics with the intention of delaying the game and as a result giving his team an unfair advantage.
• An *offside* violation.

**FOUL**

Intentional tripping

Pushing

Use of elbow

Dangerous play

*Common fouls.*

## Free Kicks

Free kicks are classified into two groups: direct and indirect. A goal can be scored directly against the offending side on a direct kick, while an indirect kick cannot be scored unless the ball is touched by a player other than the kicker before crossing the goal line between the uprights and under the crossbar.

Opponents must remain at least 10 yards from the ball until it is played. The ball is considered in play after it has traveled the distance of its own circumference (27-28 inches), and it must be stationary when the kick is taken. If the kicker plays the ball a second time before it has been touched by another player, an indirect free kick is awarded to the opposing team from the spot where the infringement occurred.

## Cautions and Ejections

When a serious violation of a law is detected, it is the responsibility of the referee to admonish the guilty party. Since the severity of fouls varies, the degree of punishment also varies.

### Yellow Card Violation.

If the referee decides to officially caution a player, he holds up a yellow card. The caution serves as a warning to the player that a repeat of the original offense, or another flagrant violation, will result in expulsion from the game.

### Red Card Violation.

When the referee decides to eject a player from the field of play, he signals by holding up a red card. A player may be sent off the field for any of the following offenses: 1) violent conduct or serious foul play, 2) foul or abusive language, 3) persistent misconduct after receiving a caution (yellow card) from the referee.

Once a player has been expelled from the game, he may not return and cannot be replaced by a substitute. The penalized team must play short-handed for the remainder of the match. The card system is an effective means of limiting violent or dangerous conduct in soccer.

## Penalty Kick

If the defending team commits a major infraction of the laws within its own penalty area, the opposition is awarded a penalty kick to be taken from the penalty mark. The goalkeeper must position between the goalposts with both feet touching the goal line. He is not permitted to move his feet until the ball has been played. A goal may be scored directly from a penalty kick. If necessary, the time of play is extended at halftime or fulltime to allow a penalty kick to be taken.

## Throw-In

When the ball passes over a sideline, either on the ground or in the air, it is put back into play by a throw-in at the point where it crossed the line. The player who takes the throw-in must face the field of play, and part of each foot must be either on the sideline or on the ground outside the sideline. The ball must be held in both hands and delivered over and from behind the head. The ball is considered "in play" as soon as it enters the field of play, and the thrower cannot touch the ball again until it has been played by another individual. A goal cannot be scored directly from a throw-in.

*Throw-in technique.*

## Goal Kick

When a ball is last touched by the (attacking) team and passes over the goal line, excluding the line between the goal-posts, either on the ground or in the air, a goal kick is awarded to the defending team. The kick is taken from within the goal area nearest to where it crossed the goal line. The ball must travel beyond the penalty area before it can be touched by another player; otherwise, the ball is not in play and the kick must be retaken. The kicker cannot touch the ball a scond time until it has been contacted by another player. Opposing players must remain outside of the penalty area until the kick is taken. A goal cannot be scored directly from a goal kick.

## Corner Kick

When the ball has last been played by the (defending) team and crosses the goal line, excluding the portion between the goal posts, either in the air or on the ground, a corner kick is awarded to the attacking team. The kick is taken from within the quarter circle marked at the nearest corner area. A goal may be scored direct from a corner kick. Opposing players must remain at least 10 yards from the ball until it is played. It is illegal for the kicker to play the ball twice in succession; it must first be touched by another player.

## Official's Signals

When the referee or linesmen observe a violation of the laws, they will signal the infraction with a variety of hand and body movements. The FIFA signals are designed to inform players, coaches and spectators of the referee's decision. The following illustrations depict the signals most often used by the officials.

** The basis for the material in this chapter was taken from the official FIFA laws.

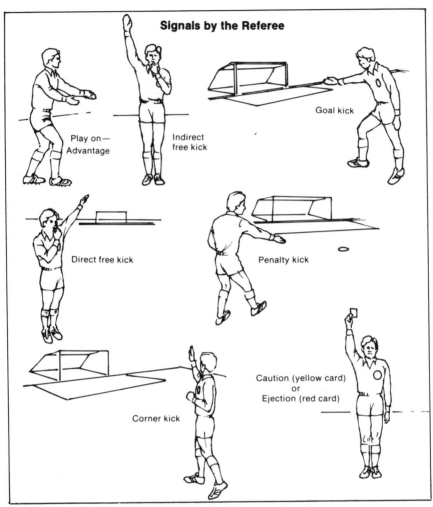

**Signals by the Referee**

Play on— Advantage

Indirect free kick

Goal kick

Direct free kick

Penalty kick

Corner kick

Caution (yellow card) or Ejection (red card)

*Official's signals - Referee.*

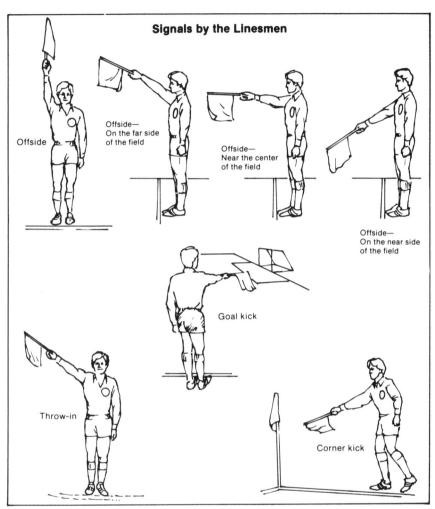

Official's signals - Linesmen.

125

# The Language of Soccer

**accelerate off the mark**  The ability to change speeds from a stationary position to full speed in the shortest possible time.

**advantage rule**  Exercised by the referee when, in his opinion, penalizing a rule infraction would give an unfair advantage to the team committing the foul. The referee instead signals continuation of play and does not call the penalty.

**agility drills**  Exercises designed to improve quickness and fluidity of movement in players.

**ASL**  American Soccer League.

**attacker**  *See* forwards.

**backheel**  Deceptive method of passing in which player steps over the ball and heels it backward to a supporting teammate.

**balance in defense**  Proper defensive positioning providing support and depth in the defense.

**ball-watching**  A common mistake among inexperienced defenders. Occurs when the defender is so intent in following the flight of the ball he forgets to mark his opponent tightly.

**banana shot**  A shot that curves in flight due to the spinning motion of the ball.

**bicycle kick**  *See* overhead kick.

**blind-side run**  Person without the ball running outside of his opponent's field of vision in order to receive a pass. A method of off-the-ball running.

**block tackle**  Using the inside of the foot to block the ball as an opponent attempts to dribble.

**catenaccio**  A defense-oriented system of play originated in Italy. Catenaccio led to low-scoring games lacking creativity and gradually gained disfavor with spectators and players alike.

**center circle**  A circle, 10 yards in radius, located at the center of the field. The initial kickoff plus restarts of play after a goal has been scored all take place in center circle.

**center forward**  Front-line attacking player occupying the central portion of the field, usually functioning as the primary goal-scoring forward.

**central striker**  *See* center forward.

**charging**  *See* shoulder charge.

**chip pass**  Method of striking the foot under the ball to direct it over an opponent to a teammate.

**circuit training**  Method of training that requires a player to complete a series of stations located within the circuit, each station consisting of drills designed to improve fitness and skill levels.

**clearance header**  A defensive heading technique. The ball is cleared out of the danger area near the goal, headed as far and as wide as possible to the wing positions.

**collecting the ball**  *See* receiving the ball.

**concentration in defense**  Defensive tactic of grouping defenders in the most dangerous areas in front of the goal, thus limiting the space available to opposing players in those critical areas.

**corner kick**  Method of putting the ball in play by the attacking team after it has crossed the opponent's end line when last touched by an opponent.

**counterattack**  Once the defending team has gained possession of the ball, it must quickly initiate its attack toward the opposing goal.

**cover**  Proper defensive support. As one defender challenges the opponent in possession of the ball, he must be supported from behind by a teammate in the event the first defender is beaten.

**cramp**  Involuntary contractions of a muscle. May be caused by a variety of reasons including, but not limited to, poor nutritional habits, fatigue, and injury to a muscle.

**defenders**  *See* fullback.

**defensive wall**  Defending players form a wall, usually composed of 3-4 players, to aid in defense against a free kick. The wall must be formed at least 10 yards from the ball.

**deflection**  Sudden change in direction of the flight of the ball.

**depth**  Proper support from behind by teammates, both in attack and defense.

**diagonal**  Run designed to penetrate the defense while drawing opponents away from their central positions.

**direct free kick**  Any free kick that can be scored directly without first touching another player.

**distribution** Methods by which the goalkeeper initiates the attack after he has gained control of the ball. The most common methods of distribution are throwing or kicking the ball to a teammate.

**diving** Technique used when a goalkeeper must leave his feet to save a shot at goal.

**drop ball** When play has been stopped by the referee for reasons other than a penalty, the play is restarted by dropping the ball between two opposing players. The ball cannot be played until it has first touched the ground.

**drop kick** Method of goalkeeper distribution in which he drops the ball and, just as it strikes the ground, kicks it downfield.

**economical training** A training scheme that incorporates fitness, skill, and tactical training within the same practice session.

**end line** Line marking the boundary at each end of the field.

**endurance training** Training regimen designed to prepare a player to function at maximum efficiency for the entire 90-minute (plus overtime) match.

**far post run** A run directed toward the far upright (goal post) on the opposite side of the field from the ball. Such a run away from the ball moves the attacker into a dangerous goal-scoring position as the ball is crossed to the far post.

**fartlek** Continuous endurance form of training consisting of long-distance running at various speeds.

**FIFA** Federation International de Football Association; the ruling body of international soccer.

**finesse** Execution of soccer skills with smoothness and precision.

**finish** The end result of every successful attack; a score.

**flexibility training** Exercises for increasing a player's range of motion.

**four-step rule** Applies to goalkeepers who are in possession of the ball. The goalkeeper is not permitted to take more than four steps when holding, bouncing, or throwing the ball without releasing it so it may be played by another player. Violation of this rule is penalized by awarding an indirect free kick to the opposition at the location where the foul occurred.

**forwards** Players who occupy the front attacking positions, usually consisting of strikers and wingers.

129

**fullbacks**  Players occupying the defensive positions in front of the goalkeeper. Most modern systems of play use four fullbacks, usually referred to as defenders.

**full volley**  Striking the ball while it is still in the air. The instep is the most common surface of the foot used in volleying.

**functional training**  Isolating the techniques and tactics of a certain playing position and stressing them in the practice session. An example of functional training for a central defender might be clearance headers to specified targets.

**give-and-go pass**  Combination passing where one player passes to another and then moves to receive an immediate return pass. Sometimes called the wall pass.

**goalkeeper**  The only player who is permitted use of the hands and arms when controlling and distributing the ball within the penalty area. His primary functions are to prevent goals by the opposition and to initiate the counterattack once he gains possession of the ball.

**goal kick**  Method of restarting play after the ball goes over the defending team's end line last touched by the attacking team. The goal kick is taken from a point 6 yards in front of the defending team's goal.

**goal side**  Proper defensive positioning. Defender must always position himself between his goal and the opponent he is marking.

**grids**  Confined areas in which soccer skills and tactics may be practiced. Reducing the playing area through the use of grids increases the difficulty of execution.

**halfbacks**  *See* midfielders.

**half volley**  Striking the ball just at the moment it touches the ground.

**heel pass**  *See* backheel.

**high pressure**  Playing style that advocates pressuring the opponents in all sections of the field. Teams applying high pressure hope to cause mistakes by the opposing team.

**indirect free kick**  A free kick from which a goal cannot be scored directly. Before entering the goal, the ball must be touched by a player other than the initial kicker.

**inside of the foot**  Area on the inside surface of the foot between the ankle and toes, used in short- and medium-range passing.

**instep** The surface of the foot covered by the laces of the shoe. Usually used for long-range passing and power shooting.

**interval training** Endurance training regimen that alternates short intervals of high-intensity work with rest intervals, a rhythm closely simulating the actual physical demands of the match.

**juggling** Using all of the various body surfaces (i.e., feet, thigh, chest, shoulders, head, etc.), except the hands, to juggle the ball in the air without allowing it to touch the ground. Juggling is often used as a warm-up exercise.

**kickboard** Wall constructed for the practice of soccer skills. The individual player may pass or shoot the ball off the wall and then receive the rebound.

**killing the ball** Taking the pace off a passed ball as you receive it.

**libero** *See* sweeper.

**linesman** One of two people who aid the referee in officiating a soccer match. One linesman is assigned to patrol each side of the field (touchline).

**linkmen** *See* midfielders.

**low pressure** Style of play that allows the opposing players time and space in which to operate in their defending and midfield zones. However, as the opposing team moves forward into the attacking third of the field, their players are more tightly marked and available space is reduced.

**man-to-man coverage** Defensive system in which each man is responsible for marking a particular opponent.

**midfielders** Players who occupy the positions in the central portions of the field. Also called halfbacks or linkmen. They connect the attack and the defense.

**mobility** Purposeful movement, both with and without the ball, serving to create space for teammates and to draw opponents into unfavorable positions.

**MISL** Major Indoor Soccer League.

**NASL** North American Soccer League.

**near-post run** Player, in an attempt to receive a pass, makes a run towards the goalpost nearest the location of the ball.

**offside position** If a player is in a technically offside position but is not interfering or involved with an opponent, the referee should not call the penalty since the player in question is not seeking to gain unfair advantage by being offside.

**offside rule**   At the instant the ball is played, a player must have two opponents, including the goalkeeper, between himself and the opposing goal; otherwise, he is offside and is penalized by an indirect free kick awarded to the opposing team. A player cannot be offside if the ball was last played by an opponent, the player is in his own half of the field, or he received the ball from a corner kick, throw-in, goal kick, or drop-ball situation.

**offside trap**   Defensive tactic in which defenders, after playing the ball upfield, quickly move forward to leave opponents in an offside position. If these opponents then receive the ball, they will be termed offside and penalized.

**one-touch passing**   Interpassing among players without stopping the ball; also called first-time passing.

**overhead kick**   Player swings both legs upward to strike the ball as it travels above his head. Also called the bicycle kick, this is a very acrobatic method of scoring goals.

**overlap**   When a team is in possession of the ball, a supporting teammate will run from behind into a forward position to receive the pass. The overlap is an excellent method of moving defenders into attacking positions for a strike at goal. Overlapping defenders typify modern soccer tactics that stress both attacking and defending capabilities in all players.

**own goal**   Occurs when a member of the defending team inadvertently directs the ball into his own goal, scoring against his team.

**passing**   Directing the ball to a teammate. Many body surfaces may be used in passing, including the inside of the foot, instep, outside of the foot, heel, toe, and head.

**penalty arc**   An arc drawn with a 10-yard radius from the penalty spot. No one, except the kicker, is allowed within the area of the arc and the penalty area when the penalty kick is being taken.

**penalty area**   Area located in front and to the sides of the goal in which the goalkeeper is allowed use of the hands in controlling the ball. The area measures 44 yards wide by 18 yards deep.

**penalty kick**   Direct free kick awarded to the attacking team if a defender commits a major foul within his own penalty area. The kick is taken from the penalty spot, located 12 yards directly in front of the goal.

**pendulum training**   Soccer ball suspended from a rope, useful for skill practice. The height of the ball may be varied for passing with the feet, heading, etc.

**penetrating pass**   *See* through pass.

**pitch**   *See* playing field.

**playing field**   Rectangular playing surface 100-130 yards long and 50-100 yards wide.

**poke tackle**   Reaching in and, using the toe, kicking the ball away from an opponent.

**possession**   Stringing together a number of passes among members of the same team; not allowing the opposition to gain control of the ball.

**punching**   The goalkeeping technique of punching balls out of the goal area. Punching is used on high air balls that the goal-keeper cannot safely catch. Rather than risk dropping the ball in the goal area, the keeper uses one or both fists to direct the ball out of the danger area.

**quick turn**   The ability of a player to receive a pass with his back to the opponent's goal, turn, and play it forward, all executed in one fluid motion.

**receiving the ball**   The art of collecting a pass and bringing it under control. The ball may be received on various body surfaces including the inside of the foot, instep, sole of the foot, outside of the foot, thigh, chest, and head.

**red card**   Presented when, in the referee's judgment, a player must be ejected from the game for violation of the rules governing play.

**referee**   The person who is responsible for officiating the soccer game. Two linesmen assist the referee.

**restarts**   Methods of beginning play after a stoppage in action. Restarts include direct and indirect free kicks, throw-ins, corner kicks, goal kicks, and the drop ball.

**rhythm**   The tempo or pace of a soccer game.

**running off the ball**   Purposeful running when not in possession of the ball to create space for teammates. Intelligent running off the ball is a requirement in modern soccer.

**save**   Goalkeeper prevents an opponent's shot from entering the goal for a score.

**scissors kick**   *See* overhead kick.

**screening**   When in possession of the ball, a player must keep his body in a position between the opponent and the ball, in effect screening his opponent. Also called shielding, this skill is very important in maintaining ball possession.

**shielding**   *See* screening.

**shin guards**   Light, protective pads worn over the front portion of the lower leg to help prevent injuries.

**shooting**   Directing the ball at the opponent's goal in an effort to score, either by kicking or heading.

**shoulder charge**   Legal tactic used when challenging an opponent for the ball.

**side volley**   Striking the ball, bouncing or traveling in the air, while it is located to the side of the player.

**slide tackle**   Method of dislodging the ball from an opponent by sliding into the ball and kicking it away.

**square pass**   A pass made across the field. Often used to slow the tempo of the game or to set up a penetrating pass.

**stamina**   Endurance; the ability to perform at a high work rate for an extended period.

**static stretching**   Method of increasing player flexibility. Muscles are stretched to their greatest extent and held in that position for 15-30 seconds. Bouncing in an attempt to increase stretching is not advisable since injury may result.

**stopper**   One of the central defenders in the standard four-man back line. The stopper usually plays in front of the sweeper and marks the opposing center forward.

**striker**   Front running, attacking player who is usually one of the primary goal scorers of the team. Also called forward.

**substitution**   Replacing a field player or the goalkeeper with another player.

**support**   Tactical term implying movement of players towards the ball to aid the teammate in possession. Proper support will provide passing options to the player in possession, likewise reducing his chances of losing the ball.

**sweeper**   The last defender, given the responsibility to support the fullback line. He sweeps behind the defense, cutting off penetrating passes to goal. Also called libero.

**systems** Organization of players on the field. Defenders are listed first, then midfielders, and finally the forwards. For example, the 4-3-3 system consists of 4 defenders, 3 midfielders, and 3 attackers. The goalkeeper is not included in the numbering.

**tackling** Using the feet to steal the ball from an opponent. *See* block table, slide tackle, poke tackle.

**tactics** Organizational concept of how individuals, groups, or an entire team of players function together.

**target man** Striker who is used as the principal target for passes originating from defenders and midfield players. The ball is played forward to the target who then distributes it to an open teammate or goes at goal himself.

**technique** Skill training; includes heading, shooting, dribbling, passing, and receiving balls.

**throw-in** Method of restarting play after the ball has traveled outside of the touchlines. Player must throw it into play using two hands directly over his head. Both feet must be kept on the ground when releasing the ball.

**total soccer** Concept of play stressing all around players who can both defend and attack. When in possession, all players attack; after loss of possession, all players defend. When playing total soccer, rigid positioning is nonexistent.

**touchline** Side boundary lines of the field. If the ball goes completely over the touchline, it is put into play by a throw-in.

**two-touch passing** Method of interpassing in which a player receiving the ball uses his first touch to control it and the second touch to pass the ball to a teammate.

**volley** *See* full volley, half volley, side volley.

**wall pass** Combination passes between two teammates. One player serves as a wall to redirect the path of the ball. The player with the ball passes off the wall and then sprints into open space to receive the return pass.

**warm-up** Exercises that physiologically prepare the body for a strenuous training session or actual match play.

**width in attack** Attacking tactic of using the entire width of the field in an attempt to draw defending players away from the central positions of the field.

**wingbacks** Fullbacks who play on the flanks of the defense, usually marking the opposing wingers.

**wingers** Forwards who operate on the flank positions near the touchlines.

**work rate** Level of physical exertion a player demonstrates throughout the game.

**World Cup** International tournament of soccer, the final games of which are held every 4 years.

**yellow card** Issued by the referee to a player who is guilty of violation of the laws concerning conduct of play during a game. A second warning (red card) constitutes ejection from the match.

**zonal defense** Defensive system in which each player is responsible for marking the opposing player(s) in a certain section of the playing field.

# Bibliography

Allen, J. Soccer for Americans. New York: Grosset & Dunlap, 1967.

Batty, Eric. Soccer Coaching the Modern Way. London: Faber and Faber, 1975.

Chyzowych, W. The Official Soccer Book of the United States Soccer Federation. New York: Rand McNally and Company, 1978.

FIFA. Laws of the Game and Universal Guide for Referees. Zurich: International Federation of Association Football, 1982.

Glanville, B. History of the World Cup. New York: Collier Books, 1973.

Harris P., and Harris, L. Fair or Foul? Manhattan Beach: Soccer for Americans, 1975.

Hughes, C. Soccer Tactics and Skills. London: British Broadcasting Corporation, 1980.

Jones, K., and Welton, P. Soccer Skills and Tactics. New York: Crown Publishers, 1977.

Luxbacher, J. Soccer: A Guide for Players, Coaches and Fans. Tulsa: Winchester Press, 1981.

Luxbacher, J., and Klein, G. The Soccer Goalkeeper: A Guide for Players and Coaches. New York: Leisure Press, 1983.

Signy, D. A Pictorial History of Soccer: London: Hamlyn House, 1968.

Suinn, R.M. Psychology in Sports. Minneapolis: Burgess Publishing Company, 1980.

U.S.S.F. Soccer Tips: How to Improve Your Skills. United States Soccer Federation, 1977.